It's Always Darkest Before the FUN Comes Up

It's Always Darkest Before the FUN Comes Up

CHONDA PIERCE

ZondervanPublishingHouse
Grand Rapids, Michigan

A Division of HarperCollins*Publishers*

It's Always Darkest Before the Fun Comes Up
Copyright © 1998 by Chonda Pierce

Requests for information should be addressed to:

📖 ZondervanPublishingHouse
Grand Rapids, Michigan 49530
ISBN 0-7394-0020-7

Published in association with the literary agency of Wolgemuth and Associates, Inc., 330 Franklin Rd., #135A–106, Brentwood, TN 37027

Interior design by Sherri L. Hoffman

Printed in the United States of America

To my husband,
David,
You make me laugh!

To our children,
Chera Kay and Zachary,
You make my life fun!
I love you very much.

CONTENTS

ACKNOWLEDGMENTS

I have such gratitude for my heavenly Father. He is indeed my everything. My heart is overwhelmed by the love and encouragement he has sent to me through these people:

- my husband—chief editor, writer, and dearest friend.
- my children—thanks for understanding every time I said, "Just wait until I finish one more chapter."
- my mother, Virginia, and my brother, Mike—this is your story too! Thanks for letting me tell it.
- Evelyn Bence—thanks for your editing, probing, and personal enthusiasm.
- my church family at World Outreach Church—your prayers and support are invaluable to me.
- my PKI friends—remember, "Preachers' kids rule!"
- my Zondervan family, especially Sandy, Sue, Mary, and Joyce—you girls sure know how to have fun!
- my incredible ministry team at Second Row Ministries—Mike and Jan Smith, I love you both! Doris Courtney, Sandy Epperson, Michelle Livingstone, RuthAnn Bowen, Robert Wolgemuth, thanks, gang!
- the pastors, conference and concert promoters, the Gaithers, the folks at Myrrh Records, radio stations and bookstore friends—you have allowed me to tell my story ... thanks for listening.

Prologue

Timing Is Everything

I'm a comedian. And I get a lot of work, actually, except at funerals. You see, before I was a comedian, I was a singer. My sister-in-law, Doris, and I had been passing out business cards for a while. She'd play the organ and I would sing. *Funerals or Weddings*, the card read. But I don't do funerals anymore. My last gig didn't go so well.

This day the funeral director, a man with hair the color of cotton, led us to a back room barely big enough for a piano and a microphone. "You'll work here," he said. "We'll pipe the music into the parlor. That way the people won't be distracted by watching you and wondering how you fit into the family."

Okay. Fine. Just pay us when we're done.

I must admit, Doris played her heart out. And I sang the old gentleman right on into heaven with a stirring rendition of "Nearer My God to Thee." (Wasn't that the same song they sang as the *Titanic* was sinking?)

We finished our selections and then waited, because we were supposed to sing one more song at the end of the service. We waited and waited. The room seemed to grow warmer and smaller, and I got bored. So I started practicing *stand-up* for my future career as a comedian. Apparently, I had a great audience! She loved me, she really loved me! I was on a roll!

Have you ever seen someone trying desperately *not* to laugh? The look on Doris's face that day was as if she were in pain and needed to relieve the pressure . . . or else. But not a sound, not a peep. Believe me, a peep would have been much better than the big blasting snort that finally broke loose.

That was it.

We lost it.

My laugh, on the other hand, is like a cackle—loud and long. So there we were—snorting and cackling, cackling and snorting. We couldn't stop!

We may have gone on like that for a long time, but in poked Cotton Head, the funeral director. He was waving both hands, trying to get our attention. "Ladies!" he called in a stage whisper, "that microphone is still on!"

Cracking the Comedy Books

I've been a student of comedy for many years now. (It sure beats chemistry—I made terrible grades in chemistry.) One of my favorite "textbooks" is a book called *Comedy Writing Secrets* by Melvin Helitzer. It has a banana-yellow cover with big letters on the front and even looks funny on the shelf. Mr. Helitzer explains a few of the terms, or formulas, used when writing a funny joke, terms like *stupidity* (that one comes pretty easy for me!), *double entendres* (play on words), *reverse* (switching the point of view), *slapstick* (catering to our delight in someone else's misfortune, like a pie in the face or laughing at someone's funeral), and *triples* (a sequence of three actions that build up the tension to an exaggerated finale). Speaking of triples . . .

I was in the fourth grade and living near the ocean in Myrtle Beach, South Carolina where my father pastored a small church. My little sister, Cheralyn, was three years younger than I and always tried to do everything I did on the monkey bars—even hang upside down. She was the first to break a bone. After the doctors had wrapped her leg in a cast that reached from the top of her leg to the tip of her toes, the folks from church lined up just to sign it. (One even wrote, "Never listen to your sister!")

A few days later my big sister, Charlotta, who was four years older than I, fell at the roller-skating rink. (Good Christian teenagers couldn't dance, but we were allowed to roller skate.) Charlotta really was graceful—on or off roller skates. But whenever she was skating there always seemed to be a lot going on: boys flying past, trying to impress her; bratty kids zipping past, teasing her about all the boys flying past. I don't really remember who caused her to trip and fall on her hand. How would I know? I was on the bottom of the pile—minding my own business.

In the emergency room the doctor explained to us that she had broken her thumb in two places. And since Charlotta was the piano-playing future of our church, the doctors wanted to be sure the break would heal properly. That meant her cast—for a broken thumb—covered her entire hand and extended way up her arm and past her elbow.

And then I had *my* "big break!"

It happened at the "big game"—the one where the coach had announced I was the shortstop, and then he told me there were only enough gloves for some of the infielders and some of the outfielders—unfortunately, I wasn't in that group. No problem. After all, this was *soft*ball. Why did we need gloves?

The first batter stepped to the plate. She was four times bigger than I (but then again, everyone at that age seemed to be four times bigger than I). Yet I straddled the *X* the coach had marked in the dirt and watched the softball move in a nice, slow arc from the pitcher to the batter. SWING! CRACK! And then the ball was coming at me—like a bullet! With my best athletic move, I planted all forty-eight pounds of me right smack dab in front of the ball.

My plan worked. Sort of. The ball smacked me in the crook of my right arm. I smothered it with my arm and the rest of my body as I dropped to my knees. What a catch! I was a hero! We won the game! Or did we? Everything after that was a blur! But when I got home, my injury was hard to hide. "Not again," Mother said, with just the slightest tinge of exasperation. "They're going to start asking questions!"

My parents decided that I should have x-rays. So Mother, Cheralyn, Charlotta, and I all piled in the car and drove to the emergency room. The x-ray confirmed Mother's worst fears: I'd broken the radius in my right arm. I'd have to wear a cast for twelve weeks. I sat quietly and watched as the white-coats wrapped my arm in strips of plaster and gauze—as if they were making a piñata.

Soon I joined Cheralyn and Charlotta in the waiting room. Cheralyn hobbled up pitifully to meet me. Charlotta adjusted her sweater, trying to hide her cast. But I waved my cast proudly—my battle scar—a war trophy!

Mother led us down the hall, a train of mummified body parts. As we passed a sitting area, I noticed a lady who had noticed us. She was well-dressed and sat with excellent posture. As we passed by I heard her say—very quaintly, very Southern—"Oh my, it's a complete set!"

The Laugh Collection

I've tried to learn a few secrets about comedy, ways to make people laugh. Because the more laughs I find, the bigger my collection gets. You see, I've actually started a laugh collection—and I could be the *only* one who does this. Some people like to collect bugs—like my eight-year-old son, Zachary, who will get an old, empty pickle jar and poke holes in the lid and set out for the backyard looking for something slimy. (And he usually finds it!) And I guess, as with any good collection, half the fun is explaining to the admirers of your collection just how you came across certain items. Zach's face just beams when he tells me how he lifted up a rotten log and chased down a centipede.

What I like about my laugh collection is that I can collect as many laughs as I want, and I never have to stick them with a pin or carry them up to the attic. And I've got thousands of them! I find them all over (except under rotten logs), from every state, every country. Sometimes I find them in my own backyard, or at the funeral home, or at the emergency room.

Sometimes, as I look over the different laughs I have collected, it's easy to see that they are so different, and they come from so many different stories or jokes. But there is something that each one of these laughs has in common. That something is *timing*.

Timing is the one thing that can make or break a funny story. *Timing is everything*. When I tell a story, I can deliver a line in a whisper, or I can yell and scream and sweat and in either instance receive a roar of laughter in return. But if I push too hard or miss the all-important pregnant pause (another comedy technique I've learned), if I rush the "zinger," the room gets so deathly quiet and still that I can hear the dust settling.

How does it work? I admit—some of it seems to come naturally. (Mothers usually recognize it early and sometimes encourage this gift by giving you a quarter to stand up on the table at Shoney's and sing a birthday song.) And some of it comes with hard work, with watching, with soaking it all in from master storytellers.

Hundreds of times I've heard Cousin Minnie Pearl talk about the time Uncle Nabob and Aunt Ambrosia were blown up through the roof when the gas furnace exploded. *Every time* I know the furnace is going to explode. *Every time* I know Uncle Nabob and Aunt Ambrosia are going to go through the roof, and *every time* I know Miss Minnie will say, "It was the first time they'd been out together in years." And I still laugh.

I've watched and learned from Miss Minnie, and I've watched and learned from some other great storytellers as well. Ken Davis can make raising teenagers actually sound fun! Dennis Swanberg can imitate the people I've always wanted to go to Sunday school with: Billy Graham, Barney Fife, and Jimmy Stewart. My friend Mark Lowry can tell a long story where virtually every line is funny. And just when I think I can't laugh any more, or harder, he'll deliver his punch line—just at the right time. Yes, there is something to this timing idea.

In another comedy textbook, *Make 'em Laugh: Life Studies of Comedy Writers*, Dr. William Fry, Jr. quotes Herbie Baker on the subject of timing: "There are no rules. Timing comes from experience—waiting for the laugh, knowing when to come in. You get a *feeling* that the timing is right. When to start telling the next joke. When performers start out they step on their own laughs. They don't wait long enough, or worse, they wait for a laugh to die down completely, then have to start building all over again."

What an incredible journey God has allowed me to take— building my collection of laughs! I'd like to say that I've always known—as Herbie puts it—when to come in, when to wait long enough. I'd like to say that I've laughed every step of the way—that only my sides have ached and not my heart (wouldn't we all!). But that wouldn't be true.

Yet, despite some unexpected storms, I'm laughing and making good timing.

I would probably argue a bit with Herbie Baker when he declares, "There are no rules." You see, I have come to realize that there is Someone who has lovingly given us guidelines, a plan that will—with his perfect sense of timing—bring us to enjoy a hearty laugh. My collection is full of many of these laughs—brought into my life with incredibly perfect timing. I find them all over, some close to home and others from far away. Like a prize marble collection, some laughs in my collection are big and some are small. Some are polished and some are roughened by wear. And, like a favorite agate, I have one laugh that is priceless. My mother gave it to me; it is the "grin after the grim." Sometimes I'll hold it up to the light, and I can see the tiny cracks that should have destroyed it long before now, and I marvel that it remains whole.

I am anxious to share this laugh with you in the pages ahead. The laugh that you may have thought was gone for good. The joy—the fun—that comes after the darkest night. That laugh may be just around the corner. So turn the page and come along with me on this journey for a while, learning how, when *God's* clock is ticking, his timing is perfect. Because, after all, timing is everything.

One

Before the Fun Comes Up

If I speak in the tongues of men and of angels, but have not love,
I am only a resounding gong or a clanging cymbal.
1 Corinthians 13:1

She wore a blue gingham dress and a flat straw hat, complete with a dangling price tag, the day I met Sarah Cannon, known to her fans as Minnie Pearl.

I sat backstage at the Grand Ole Opry, twenty-three years old, newly married, still trying to decide what I wanted to be when I grew up. I was pretty mad at the world. You see, life had not turned out the way I had wanted it to. I wanted everything to be fun and hilarious (not too unrealistic in my expectations, was I?). But instead I had to deal with pain, grief, disillusionment—things I never would have ordered for myself. And it was tough trying to be funny on the outside (just to get a paycheck) when nothing seemed very funny to me on the inside. I was angry. Resentful. But I believed I was doing an incredible job of hiding all of that.

Until Miss Minnie came along.

I had gotten a job at Opryland, USA by auditioning along with thousands of other young people. I was cast in a show called "Country Music, USA" with fifteen other kids about my age. Six days a week we would dress up like country music stars from the past and the present and put on a show that was high-energy and full of music, song, and dance. Yes, dance. And for a preacher's kid who had barely been to the prom, this was a problem.

But the director solved it quickly: he gave me a straw hat with a price tag on it and said, "Do you think you'd like to tell some jokes?"

So, every show, while the rest of the cast clogged about the old wooden stage, I changed into a Minnie Pearl costume and prepared for a grand entrance and a giant "Howdee!" at the end of the song.

The Real Thing

One week during the summer, our cast was scheduled to perform for a special event at the Grand Ole Opry House. The John Deere folks were in town, and who better to entertain them than a group of kids who sounded like the real stars? I don't think any of us were especially excited about singing in a circle of tractors and lawn mowers. We even had to change a few dance steps (those who danced, anyway), because at any given moment, the latest green-and-yellow mower would come zipping by. (Maybe they cut grass really well, but they are also very quiet, sneaky machines.) But this was our opportunity to be on the stage of the world-famous Grand Ole Opry, appearing with Whispering Bill Anderson. And, of course, the extra hundred dollars in our paychecks wasn't bad either!

I learned a lot (everything I knew) about the history of country music that summer—especially since I was impersonating such greats as Mabel Carter (autoharp), Martha Carson (guitar), and Barbara Mandrell (shiny clothes). Even though the autoharp and shiny clothes were fun, I really got excited when it came time for me to adjust the price tag on my hat and walk out onto that stage in front of that packed auditorium, especially during these two special shows.

These were different from all other shows because, as the music was fading, I was to step out onto the stage and holler, "Howdee!" But before the audience could respond with the traditional echo, the REAL Cousin Minnie Pearl would step out onto the stage and playfully ask me, "Well, who are you?!" I would then proudly introduce the real Minnie Pearl to the audience and girlishly skip offstage.

That night and the next, I stood transfixed in the wings and watched Miss Minnie weave a tale from Grinder's Switch that magically transported these businessmen to a country porch where the funniest things happen to the simplest people.

So that's who I'm pretending to be, I thought, looking at Miss Minnie past the price tag that dangled from my own hat. And that seemed okay with me.

"Who Are You?"

I'd be lying if I said that none of us was starstruck at being backstage of the famous Grand Ole Opry. Photos hung in rows along the walls of the hallway, usually black-and-whites of men with hair slicked back, like Stonewall Jackson and Porter Wagoner, and women with big hair like Dolly Parton and Loretta Lynn. Doors with stars glued in the center led off the hallway into tiny dressing rooms paneled in mirrors surrounded by light bulbs. It was fun to watch my friends gawk—at the photos, at the mailboxes with names like Acuff and Mandrell taped to the front, at the carpet where the feet of many of the people we were impersonating had walked regularly. We were just kids, and this was big, BIG time.

When I wasn't watching Miss Minnie onstage, I was studying her backstage in dressing room one. Miss Minnie was open and kind. Eight of us (more than that if you counted all the reflections in the mirrors) surrounded her as she shared some stories about her early years when she traveled around the country and overseas with the likes of Roy Acuff and Patsy Cline.

Backstage her voice was soft and sophisticated. She had an air of success about her, yet she was humble and kind. When she'd talk to us, she'd look directly into our faces—sometimes right at me—yet she never made us feel uncomfortable, intimidated, or unworthy. Rather, she made us feel as if we were in the living room of her home. I watched her as she meticulously tucked her hair under her hat, dabbled a bit of powder across her nose, and before my very eyes, Sarah Cannon was transformed into the fun-loving country bumpkin, Cousin Minnie Pearl from Grinder's Switch, Tennessee.

Moments before our last "duet," she and I stood alone behind the curtain and waited for our cue. At that point in my life, very few professional colleagues knew anything about the layers of pain I was wearing around my heart. I can't see how Miss Minnie could have picked me out of those eight girls in the dressing room as the one carrying the greatest load of pain. I really thought I had disguised it so well.

Yet, as we stood in the soft edges of light that spread from center stage, she leaned closer to me and whispered, "Do you like this kind of thing?" She was talking to me, looking only at me. I didn't have to share her with a tiny room full of others. And it was obvious that "thing" meant performing, being on stage, making people laugh.

"Yes, ma'am," I answered quickly.

I was surprised by her question. Even more so, I was surprised she was even talking to me. I had always thought performers had to meditate, bite their nails, do something to prepare them for the big entrance. Not today. Miss Minnie was just calm and collected, certain of her lines, her job. I was the one biting fingernails!

Then, never looking away from my eyes, she said, "Well, you gotta love people to make 'em want to laugh." She told me an old story of advice given to her when she was just starting out: "Love 'em, and they'll love you back." The message was clear: Love your audience, girl. Then, almost as if she were looking right into my heart, she said, "And you really won't know anything about laughing until you have found peace with God and love him first."

Suddenly the stage manager nodded. (Minnie, the old pro, had kept track of him, out of the corner of her eye.) That was our cue. So with Minnie's words still settling into my ears, I stepped onto the stage and up to the microphone and shouted as loudly as I possibly could, "HOWDEE!"

And then came the playful answer, which suddenly took on a more serious twist: "Well, who are you?!"

When the show ended, I ran to the dressing room to find Miss Minnie, but by the time I could get changed, she had already gone. I don't know what I would have said to her. Perhaps I just needed another glance at her face, another look into her eyes. Perhaps I wanted to know if my mother had called her and asked her to poke at my heart and remind me she was praying for my aching soul, trying to hurry the time along toward healing.

"You gotta love people to make 'em want to laugh.... And you really won't know anything about laughing until you have found peace with God and love him first."

There was something perfect about Miss Minnie's words— and their timing in my life. She had found me waiting backstage in the dark, longing to enjoy a good laugh. How could she have known that what I was doing was standing, waiting, with my heart craning toward the slightest bit of light, longing to feel the morning sun across my face? How could she have known, in the darkest of my days, that what I was doing was waiting for the *fun to come up?*

But I'm getting ahead of myself. Let me go back to the beginning to tell you how I got to where I am now and how, eventually, Miss Minnie's words set in motion a process that helped me find the fun, the fun that comes after the darkest night.

Two

The Curtain Rises

Weeping may remain for a night, but rejoicing comes in the morning.
Psalm 30:5

My mother tells me I have always been a cutup. When I was three, she would stand me on the coffee table during Sunday school parties, and I'd sing my own version of "Bringing in the Sheaves." (Don't you miss the old hymns!?) My arrangement was a tap-dance version very similar to Shirley Temple's "Good Ship Lollipop!" except I would sing "Bringing in the sheep!" (I think that song would still be in the hymnal if the church had simply adopted my version!)

Mother took me from one audition to the next. One year I was voted Little Miss Horry County in Myrtle Beach, South Carolina. I won a trophy, twenty-five dollars, and a chance to wear my new tiara in the Sun Fun Parade. I practiced my plastic grin and mechanical wave for weeks!

When I was eight, I auditioned for a part in *The Music Man* being performed at the Civic Center by the Myrtle Beach City Drama Troupe. I got the part of Gracie Shinn (the mayor's youngest daughter). I only had two lines, but I put my whole heart into each: "Papa! Papa! The Wells Fargo Wagon is coming up from the depot! and I know who did it. Tommy did it. That's who."

Ironically, my freshman year of college I again played in *The Music Man*, this time as Zaneta Shinn (the mayor's oldest daughter). I was disappointed. I wanted the same role I'd had when I was eight because I still had those lines memorized!

Most of the roles I played weren't on the "real stage." They just fell into my lap. Some I really enjoyed (like playing "The Mod Squad" with my friend; I played the character Pete) and others that weren't so fun (like consoling Cheralyn when we moved away because Dad had taken a new church). But whatever the part, I was always up for it. It didn't take me long to realize that when it came to playing a role, I was a natural.

Act I: To Grandmother's House We Go

For as long as I can remember, every summer my parents would take us to Nanny's for at least a week, sometimes more, sometimes almost the whole summer. We said good-bye to Mom and Dad, who'd go back home to attend to the business of the church. I always thought it was too bad they weren't able to stick around and enjoy the show.

Since we lived in South Carolina most of my childhood and my maternal grandparents (Nanny and Papaw) lived in Kentucky, we didn't get to see them often. So when we finally did, there was cause for celebration—or at least a show! And my older sister, Charlotta, was the best at scripting and directing a living-room production. With just a simple white sheet draped across a fishing line, we would transform Nanny's living room into a stage; the front room, usually dark and filled with big, clunky furniture covered with a paisley fabric, would be the site of the Courtney Family Frolics!

On the day of the show, we'd work all day practicing our lines, memorizing important passages, blocking the stage directions—it was important to know if we should enter from "sheet" right or left, or just push through the slit in the middle.

A typical show would begin with my brother, Michael, blaring out a tune on his trumpet—something like a cross between *How Great Thou Art* and *Won't You Come Home, Bill Bailey?* Then Charlotta would drag a rocker in front of the sheet and pretend to be sewing on one of Nanny's quilts while doing a dramatic, patriotic monologue, as if she were Betsy Ross. Then Mike would reappear, stand down stage, and recite from memory the Gettysburg Address. (It took me a while, and several history classes, to figure out that Betsy Ross and Abraham Lincoln did not know each other.) Cheralyn, the youngest, just did whatever we'd tell her to do. Usually that meant holding up the handmade posters with big block letters that read ACT I or ACT II. And me? I'd sing all the goofy songs of course: "Hey, Look Me Over" (complete with Hobo costume), or my favorite lyric in the world: *Mares eat oats, and does eat oats.* . . . Those songs lasted until more sophisticated solos came along, like "Jeremiah was a bull frog" ("Joy to the World").

Then, once all the solo performances were complete, we'd clear the stage and prepare for the ensemble. We'd sing this song called "I Wanna Be Ready," complete with harmony and choreography, all orchestrated by Betsy Ross, I mean, Sis. We'd begin with our backs to the audience (which usually consisted of Nanny and Papaw and maybe an aunt or uncle and cousin or two). Michael started with a deep (as deep as a fifteen-year-old can get) "I wanna be ready," as he spun around on his heels to face the audience. (I think it's something Charlotta had seen the Jackson Five do on the *Ed Sullivan Show!*) Then Charlotta, with the alto line. Then Cheralyn. Then I would belt out the same line, dropping to one knee, in a voice so high and sharp that Nanny and Papaw would rock back at the same instant. This program seemed to go over so well in Nanny's living room that we decided to take it home to our congregation (without the bullfrogs and mares, of course!). Dad even bought a couple of new microphones.

Not long after that, Mike's voice began to change. Some days he was a bass, some days a tenor. Cheralyn was still too young and shy to want sing with us (plus she liked the job of holding up the signs), so Charlotta and I teamed up with two other girls from the neighborhood and formed a group we called The Power and Light Company. Mom went to the fabric store one day and bought enough bright red polyester to make four dresses that looked just alike (another reason Mike left the group). She made some white coordinating vests that glittered just enough to make us feel as if we could compete with the Supremes! (Of course we could never sing *Stop! In The Name Of Love* at church, but we looked good!)

Our visits to Nanny's were the most memorable occasions in my childhood. When we weren't putting on a show in Nanny's living room, we were outside, at the farm—doing farm stuff. Papaw had a garden, a big one. We'd all trail after him with something sharp to dig weeds or with a bucket to pick vegetables. And if I happened to get hungry while I worked, or the smell of fresh tomatoes became too tempting, I'd just pluck one of the ripe fruits from a plant, rub a spot clean, and eat the tomato right there—bugs and all—just like I'd seen Papaw do.

And the best ride on the big farm was not the old milk cow in the barn or the crazy horse that roamed the pasture, but the old white propane tank in the backyard. The big metal cylinder on four legs was parked beneath the trees, and we'd ride it "all over the prairie," through dusty towns and grassy fields. Sometimes I would get a running start and jump onto its back and ride away just before the posse could catch me. Other times I'd slide off its round back and announce that there was a new sheriff in town. Sometimes Papaw would bring us ice-cold watermelon, and we'd line up on the back of this tank and not worry about eating manners at all. Sticky watermelon juice would be all over us and the old propane tank. First it would be so slippery we could hardly stay on. Cheralyn would giggle. But soon it would turn sticky and we could hardly get free.

Papaw's garden was on the other side of the house, but around the propane tank, watermelon plants would sprout up, growing like weeds in a tangle. But Papaw just let them grow—and we were proud of them.

Back home our imaginations still kept us girls entertained for hours. When Charlotta wasn't busy orchestrating a living-room show, she was the cruise director of *The Love Boat*. Cheralyn and I would always take a trip—mainly for the meals. Charlotta would serve us bologna and tomatoes, but she would lay out the silverware as if this were a six-course meal.

"No, no, no. That's not the right fork," Charlotta would say if I picked up the one that was placed parallel (or was it perpendicular?) to the soup spoon. The tomato was our salad and Charlotta would serve, watch, and then grade us on our manners. (Extra credit was given if we extended a pinky whenever we sipped our Kool-Aid.) No one ever fell in love on our Love Boat, but we did learn the proper way to fold a napkin.

I don't know the exact day that it happened. But eventually Charlotta was too old, too proud, and too much a teenager to play make-believe with us anymore. For some reason she began to notice "yucky" boys, and playtime was over for her. She was too busy painting her finger nails and restyling her hair to ever play silly games with the "little girls" (as Charlotta referred to us!).

Act II: Mom Gets Us Ready

Mom had these big cat-eye glasses that made her face look tiny. She was the perfect preacher's wife: she played the piano, she led the ladies fellowship, she could bake a pie, she wrote all the Vacation Bible School programs, and she produced the Christmas play every year. She had also given birth to four kids who were soon old enough to bring the special music any Sunday it was needed.

I always remember Mom busy getting things ready, whether it was a Sunday school program or just us kids. For a while Dad hosted a live Sunday morning radio show that aired early—real early. Mom would make sure we were all bathed Saturday night and then, as we lay in bed—sometimes after we had fallen asleep—she would take bobby pins and roll our hair into little finger curls and pin them tight to our heads. (This may be why Mike got a haircut like Dad's.)

Then early Sunday morning, Mom would shuffle us all to the car—still in our pajamas—and we'd drive to the radio station. We (The Power and Light Company—with Mike and Cheralyn) would sing, and Dad would preach. While he was bringing Myrtle Beach the text from God's Word, Mom would be taking out the bobby pins and helping us get dressed for church—right there in the radio station.

Mom always wanted things to be right—to be pleasing—for her family and her church family, from the little pin curls in our hair to the amount of sugar in someone's iced tea. Mom was always trying to help anyone in need. So when there was the accident in the church, Mom was right there to help (and to make sure we didn't laugh—which would have made the guest preacher uncomfortable).

Brother Harold Liner came in as a special evangelist one Sunday. He was an energetic outgoing man with a strong voice and some very animated gestures when he'd preach. He was preaching this one Sunday and got so blessed at the Word that he began to jump and move about in the pulpit. Since we had many, many productions at our church—Mom was very prolific with programs—she had decided it was much more convenient to leave the clothesline wire running from one side of the platform to the other, than to take it down every time. And of course, the secret to good staging is to hide all the hardware. I don't think Brother Liner ever knew what hit him (or undercut him). He went up and then went down, and then went horizontal—right out on the floor! (We were all too stunned to laugh then. First we wanted to make sure he was still alive.) Dad fired off a dismissal prayer and ended the service. He then led Brother Liner to the parsonage, and Mom did a first-rate bandaging job.

Perhaps that is the moment she was first inspired to become a nurse! While we were still in South Carolina, Mother would drive a hundred miles round trip to Columbia to nursing school. For over a year she did this. Part of my role that year was to work the flashcards. Mom would be on one side of the table, Cheralyn and I on the other. I'd flip a card that would have the name of some hard-to-pronounce member of the penicillin family, and she'd pronounce it! (I think, anyway.) And then we'd take a break and watch her stick needles in oranges and draw out 5cc of orange juice.

I didn't know why Mother wanted to be a nurse. There was plenty to keep her busy just playing the piano and working on productions at the church.

With school, church, four children to raise, and life with her husband—I don't know when Mom ever slept. And as we moved into our teen years, things didn't get much easier for her. She wanted us to be happy, to feel special, sheltered—now I know that many of those sleepless nights were spent praying for all of us.

Act III: Dad Gets a New Suit

For a long time I remember my dad sporting a flat-top hair-cut and wearing his black horn-rimmed glasses. (Of course, I think all glasses were black horned-rimmed in the late '60s.) He was always intense—busy—and finding different ways to serve the Lord. He was a fairly young man—somewhere in his thirties—when we were living in Glens Fork, Kentucky. (I was about eight.) One winter night, so late that we had all gone to bed, someone knocked on the door of the parsonage and woke us all up. Dad answered the door, and a man with messy hair and clothes swayed in the doorway, mumbling that he wanted to be baptized. Dad kept asking the guy questions, trying to confirm the request. Mom huddled us together, and we heard Dad speaking and the man moaning. Finally, Dad took him by the arm and said, "Okay, if you want to be baptized, I'll do it for you and right now." Together they left.

We all raced to a window to watch them walk (stagger) the short distance to the church next door. But instead of going to the church, Dad led our visitor to the small creek behind our house. It was so cold that a thin sheet of ice had formed. Dad broke it in with the heel of his shoe and gave the man a blessed dunking right there. The next morning Mother and Dad just chuckled about their new convert (those chuckles are in my collection) and marveled at how fast ice water can sober a man. (We never saw him again.)

But Dad was like that. If something needed to be done, he'd do it—and usually right then. I was about nine years old when we moved to Myrtle Beach. We hadn't been there long when Cheralyn and I decided we needed a clubhouse. We found an old dumpsite not far from the house and scavenged some boards and window screens. We dragged it all to our backyard. Because neither of us could drive a nail, we just leaned one piece against another. When we had everything in place, we crawled in through an opening and hoped it didn't cave in on us.

Dad wasn't real happy with our construction site, so he took matters into his own hands. "If you're gonna do this," he said, "I want it to be right." We got excited because we knew Dad had a hammer, and he knew how to use it. He drove to the hardware store, bought some real lumber, and built us a square with a roof on it. He then cut out holes for the window panes, and Cheralyn and I painted on frames complete with flowering window boxes. In only one afternoon, Dad built us a first-rate clubhouse.

Dad also did those "dad" kind of things—like help his kids buy their first car. He helped Charlotta buy a 1966 Corvair (they were sharp cars back then) and helped Mike get a Rambler (an old one). When I was old enough, he helped me to buy a brand-new car! (I think he got tired of keeping the others running.) It was a 1978 Datsun F-10, small, sporty, with a stick shift. (I made the payments from my two part-time jobs.)

But none of those were as fun (or as cool) as Dad's motorcycle—a Honda CB125 (real cool).

Dad's skills as a mechanic were also needed to help keep our mini-fleet of automobiles running smoothly—or at least running. And somehow I became his number-one mechanic. (I think that was because I was the only one to complete the training course. He taught me the difference between a Phillips and a flathead screwdriver.) On work day, I would position myself somewhere between the toolbox and the car and wait for a greasy hand to reach out from beneath the Corvair and for a voice to say, "Pliers." Within seconds I'd slap a pair into his palm. But this wasn't exactly the easiest job in the world. I always seemed to be confusing a 5/8 boxed-end wrench with a 9/16 open-end. (And holding the flashlight still for someone changing a spark plug is a skill I don't think any preteen has ever possessed.) I used to think that my confusing the wrenches is what sometimes caused him to be in a bad mood.

Dad was a doer. He was always busy—preaching, building shelves, building cabinets and clubhouses, working on cars, buying cars, saving souls, and baptizing them. He was so busy that sometimes instead of changing into some work clothes, he'd roll up the sleeves of his dress shirt and mow the lawn, his dress tie flapping like the flag waving above our clubhouse. Dress shirt, tie, dress slacks—always, everywhere.

So when I was a teen and I first noticed changes in Dad's wardrobe—he was wearing a white suit with white shoes—I thought maybe he was experimenting with a fashion trend. But then there also was the hair. He was growing it a little bit longer and combed back. What was this about? At the time I wasn't quite sure.

But I sensed my mother was praying harder and longer.

Act IV: The Setting Changes

Too bad we weren't able to collect some frequent mover's miles when I was growing up. Charlotta was born in Fort Campbell, Kentucky. I was born in Covington, Kentucky. Cheralyn, the baby, and Mike, the oldest, were born in Beech Grove, Indiana. (Don't ask me how that happened!) Then there was a year or two in Rock Hill, South Carolina; a few in Georgetown, South Carolina; a brief stop in Glens Fork, Kentucky; five years in Myrtle Beach, South Carolina; a few years in Orangeburg, South Carolina. And it seemed we never knew when we were moving. Mom and Dad did, but we kids would just get the information one morning as we were heading out for school: "By the way, we're moving this week, so make sure you turn in your library books."

I hated to leave Myrtle Beach the most. That's where I'd found my best friend, Donna Thompson. We rode bikes together, played softball together, and put many criminals behind bars (not to mention the times we saved the world from complete destruction by some mad scientist). In our minds, we were *The Mod Squad*, but we drove *Starsky and Hutch*'s red car!

I was never sure if it was just the nature of Dad's job that required we moved a lot or that it just took each church a few years to get to know us—but we moved and often. Our last move was to Tennessee when I was fifteen. Part of the reason we moved to Ashland City, a little town just outside of Nashville, was to be closer to Mike and Charlotta, who were attending a college in Nashville.

In Ashland City, Dad took a little church that, as always wherever Dad went, began to experience a steady growth. The congregation of about forty soon grew to over a hundred. Charlotta, the pianist, was helping Mom, the organist, with productions, and Mike was leading the music. Our experience with some earlier living-room shows was paying off. (Cheralyn could have even stepped forward and held up a sign printed ACT I.)

In 1976, everything was red, white, and blue in honor of the country's bicentennial celebration. In Ashland City, someone had the idea of putting together a community youth choir of teenagers from churches all over town. More than twenty young people practiced for a production of *Ring All the Bells of Freedom* that was to debut at the county fair grounds on July 4 and then be produced again at a half dozen churches in town over the following weeks.

And guess who that *someone* was? Charlotta—Sis. She took charge of choir direction, stage direction, costuming (everything was red, white, and blue—how hard could that be?), and even printing up the programs. She designed her own dress of course—a modern-day Betsy Ross! We practiced for hours all the patriotic songs and the side steps and the marching on and off stage, waving our flags, and shaking our sparklers. Before every practice, Charlotta would read a devotion and pray. After every practice, I was so proud to be an American—and Charlotta's little sister.

Someone donated a big roll of butcher paper, and we made posters announcing the event and hung them in churches and businesses all over town. A local water heater manufacturer donated several giant boxes, and we turned them into marble columns. (That seemed pretty patriotic.)

By Saturday, July 3, we were as ready as we would ever be. We were just praying that the weather would cooperate.

Charlotta had to go to work so she hurried about that morning, mentally and verbally checking off a list of things to do. She gave Cheralyn and me a tall stack of inky smelling papers and said, "Make sure you get all these programs folded. I'll be back later." No problem.

Dad had left to take Mom to the Cut-N-Curl to get her hair fixed. (Always on Saturday—ready for Sunday!) Mike was off on a camping trip. Cheralyn and I folded programs for a bit and then

Dad honked his horn in the driveway. He was playing taxi that morning. He had dropped Mother off and now it was my turn. I was working part-time for my cousin Jerry Huff who ran an insurance office next to Shirley's Bakery. Dad dropped me off, and as I unlocked the office door, the phone rang. It was Cheralyn. "What's the matter," I said. "Tired of folding already?"

"No. Someone from the sheriff's office called looking for Mom or Dad. I was trying to catch him. Something's wrong. There's been an accident." I told her I'd call the Cut-N-Curl, and when I got Mom on the phone, she already knew something was wrong. They had to get to General Hospital. "Lock up the office. We're coming by to pick you up," she said hurriedly. In a matter of minutes I heard the horn from Dad's Ford. I ran out and jumped in the back seat. I could tell by the scarf around Mother's curlers that she hadn't finished at the beauty shop. I would have made my usual crack, "New do, Mom?" But the silence in the car was choking my words.

Dad whipped into the driveway at home. "Stay here with Cheralyn, and we'll call you when we get to the hospital."

While Cheralyn and I waited, I sat down at the piano and played a few notes. Charlotta's *Ring All the Bells of Freedom* book was lying there on top of the piano. The director's copy, of course. She had wedged it into a giant songbook to mark the page. In the songbook I turned open that page and immediately recognized the song—which she had sung at church on Wednesday night: "Whatever It Takes."

Suddenly, a wave of sadness swept over me, and a tear fell down my face. Cheralyn noticed and said, "Chonda, what's wrong?"

"Nothing. It's just a good song, that's all." I squared my shoulders, but somehow, I knew. I just knew. And within the hour Dad called and told us that Charlotta had been in a bad car accident. Charlotta was dead.

There was no community youth choir performance at the fairgrounds on July 4 that year. However, the participants all wore their red, white, and blue outfits to Charlotta's funeral. She lay like a princess in a flower garden, adorned in the most beautiful patriotic dress. Beside her we laid her book, *Ring All the Bells of Freedom*—the director's copy.

About a month later, Michael organized the group back together, and we performed the concert at our church—just like Sis had taught us.

Act V: Exit—Stage Left

Over a year went by—like a blur to me. Because Charlotta had been away at college, sometimes I believed that she was just going to walk in the door at any moment. But most of the time I knew she wasn't. To my friends and to people in the community, I'm sure life appeared to be carrying on well for us. Dad preached, Mom played the piano, Mike would lead the singing, Cheralyn and I would sing specials. But our wounds were deep, and we just kept them covered with some of those Looney Tune Band-Aids that made everyone think "Yeah, yeah. They're going to be all right. He's a preacher, and all those kids grew up in the church."

But either the walls at my house grew thinner or Mom and Dad just got louder. In the daytime and at night, I listened to the sounds of a marriage breaking apart.

In the fall of 1977, Cheralyn and I were going to high school together, and Michael had fallen in love and was going to marry the best piano player in the world, Doris. (Really, it's true, in the whole world!) Their wedding was set for November 19. Dad was doing the ceremony. Mom was planning the reception.

The wedding was beautiful. Doris wore a gorgeous Victorian gown with a large-brimmed hat. We had family come in from South Carolina. Nanny and Papaw sat with mother. I sang "You Light Up My Life," and Cheralyn stood patiently at the door welcoming guests, asking them to sign their names and passing out tiny little bags of rice to each guest. The wedding went off without a hitch— except for the slight incident during the wedding prayer. When Mike and Doris knelt at the altar with their backs to the congregation, the congregation noticed the simple message someone had painted across the soles of Michael's shoes in bold, white letters:

"HELP ME!" (Can't imagine who would have done such a thing!) At the reception, we ate cake and sipped punch. People laughed and chuckled. Mike threw the garter and Doris threw the bouquet. It was official: Doris was now my new sister.

I'm not sure what other families do after weddings—eat, dance, pose for photographs? But as Mike and Doris drove out of town with silly messages painted on their car (can't imagine who did that either!), my dad congratulated everyone, drove to the house, loaded up his suitcase, and then drove away—in *my* car!

I remembered some of the things I'd seen—usually when I wasn't supposed to. I remembered some of the things I'd heard—usually while holding Cheralyn as she heard the same things and cried.

No one told me, but I sensed what was happening that November day, especially when I saw Mother cry as Nanny held her close.

Three days later, Mike called home from his honeymoon to see how we were, and I heard Mother on the telephone use the *divorce* word for the first time. Mike and Doris immediately drove home, and within hours Mike was sitting at the dining room table telling Mother, Cheralyn, and me the only thing he could say: that we would be all right; not to worry.

"Things fall apart," wrote poet William Butler Yeats. That year my life started to unravel. So we got some more Looney Tune Band-Aids and I reassessed my role: now *I* was the big sister. Some nights I would sleep with Cheralyn and console her as she would cry herself to sleep. I didn't like this role at all.

We made ourselves count our blessings: we had a home, we had mom, we had Tippy (a poodle), and mostly we had each other. Only a few months later, Cheralyn and I were practicing our lines for the all-school play and managing to have some fun.

And when I finally got the nerve and confessed to Mother who the *someone* was who had written on the soles of Michael's wedding shoes, we all laughed together.

Three

The Final Curtain Call

Even in laughter the heart may ache, and joy may end in grief.
Proverbs 14:13

When I performed for drama groups and in school plays, the *Ahhh*s were always nice, but I remember when I fell in love with the laughs.

It was my senior year in high school and opening night of the all-school play. My whole family—Mom, Nanny, Aunt Ruth, Thad, Jerry, Ann, Uncle Gerald and Aunt Bonnie, and a few cousins I didn't even know we had—occupied the front few rows of our high school theater to catch our version of Rodgers and Hammerstein's classic *Oklahoma!* The story is set on the prairie of Oklahoma, just at the time the territory is about to become a state. Curly and Laurey are the main characters. (The audience knows that the two love each other long before they ever do.) Judd Fry is the bad guy who loves Laurey but can't have her.

My favorite line in this story comes right after the handsome Curly pledges his undying love for Laurey. He bends to one knee, with cowboy hat over his heart. As the music for the song "People Will Say We're In Love" begins to swell, he asks, "Please, Laurey, can't you think of some reason you might wanna marry me? Please, ma'am?"

Rather coyly and distractedly she responds, "Nope! Can't think of none right now hardly!"

And the crowd just *roared*. Wow!

Did I tell you that I was Laurey?

And that was it—my earliest remembrance of loving the sound of a roaring laugh. For me, it never compared with the sigh issued during the breadth of a romantic interlude or the sniffle heard in the hush of a dramatic pause; the laughter was ten times better. From then on I was hooked. I loved the laughs, and I loved to cause them.

Nine performances later, I was milking my favorite line for all it was worth, using my best Southern twang. I don't think Rodgers and Hammerstein intended *Oklahoma!* as a comedic masterpiece, but for me it was.

My Shadow

Cheralyn, who was in the ninth grade, had been a bit disappointed after the *Oklahoma!* auditions. She had hoped to get the part of Ado Annie, a rather silly young woman who might be called the "supporting actress." Instead, she had been cast to be my counterpart in a dream ballet scene. At one point in the play, Laurey falls asleep and dreams of herself and Curly gliding about gracefully doing some ballet moves right there on the farm. (A scene like this would have great comedy potential for me. Maybe that's why no one would let me do it!) But Cheralyn was naturally graceful. She moved like a breeze and turned like a feather being blown. Only blue lights shone as she twirled, sending her blue gingham dress out in a pleated fan. Just off stage I'd watch her, her blonde hair twirling and falling in sync with the gingham. She moved about like I could have only done in a dream. I was so proud of her.

Her partner was a young man named David Pierce. He was a senior like me and didn't live too far away, so he'd drive over often, and together they'd practice the run and lift—over and over and over in our living room. Even after the performances had begun, she would still want to practice. So David would come over and help keep her on her toes.

There was a tradition in our little theater that with every play the actors would write their names on the backstage block walls and just below it the part they had played. One night I took a big marker and wrote my name and just below that "Laurey." Cheralyn wrote, not too far away, "Cheralyn. Laurey ballet." In the play she was my double, my shadow, a dream vision of me. She could have resented this role: the spotlight would shine whenever I was on stage, and she would dance in the shadows, but she fell in love with the part. And backstage we would often stand side by side in our blue dresses—we were sisters.

Our small town was soon abuzz with what was going on at the high school theater. *Oklahoma!* was a hit all over again. We were only supposed to do four performances, but people kept calling, and people kept coming. Through it all, my favorite line never changed. I knew that some of the people were coming again and again (my cousin Thad), yet every time the laughs would still be there. We were having so much fun singing, dancing, dressing like cowboys and prairie women. Judd Fry would step out on stage and make people hiss, then he'd step behind the sheet—I mean, curtain—and we'd all laugh at how much fun we were having putting on a show. We did ten shows before the fun ended.

"I Don't Feel So Good"

During the ninth show, during one of those hushed moments when everyone backstage whispers (possibly when Judd was plotting evil so that Laurey would fall in love with him), I saw Cheralyn lean against the wall. She exhaled with a sigh and told me, "I don't feel so good." "Just a little nervous probably," someone else whispered. She grinned and moments later stepped out into the blue light and moved about like a whisper.

The next day was Saturday, and Cheralyn stayed in bed. She really wasn't feeling well. She had a fever and was coughing a lot. "Just rest," we told her. She had put so much of herself into this play that she was totally exhausted. She didn't want to miss this last show. She couldn't stand it, but Mom would not let her out of bed. Her understudy would dance the last dance. When I came home that night, I tiptoed into her room to tell her all she had missed: striking the set, hugging the cowboys and saying good-bye to everyone in the cast. But she was already asleep. I figured she would have to say good-bye later.

By Sunday her fever was still there, only now she was having trouble keeping her food down. Mom talked to the family doctor, who phoned in a prescription for antibiotics. Because Mom—a licensed practical nurse—was working the night shift at a nearby nursing home, I was in charge of getting up in the night to check on Cheralyn's fever. "Try to get her to drink some water every few hours," Mom instructed.

The antibiotics hadn't worked by Monday, and by Tuesday it was obvious that they weren't going to. Cheralyn was getting weaker; she could hardly sit up in bed. I decided to sleep with her that night and had fallen asleep when I was awakened by a loud "thump" in the hallway. I discovered Cheralyn's side of the bed was empty. But out in the hallway, there she was collapsed on the floor. I don't know how I did it, but I scooped her up off the floor and carried her to her bed. I then called Mom and told her that Cheralyn had fainted. She was only out for a little while, and Mom and the doctor showed up at about the same time. He gave Cheralyn a shot of something and told Mother he was going to make her an appointment with a specialist thirty miles away in Nashville as soon as they could work her in. Wednesday and Thursday we gave her aspirin and water and stroked her fevered face with a wet cloth. What was taking them so long? Mom was still going to work, and I was still sleeping by Cheralyn's side.

That Friday morning Mom and I drove Cheralyn to the specialist. Cheralyn got to wear her pajamas and lay in the backseat with a pillow, just like we used to do on long trips. I missed school that day. If they were going to give her a shot, I had to be there to make sure she was going to be all right.

Dr. Spiegel was with Cheralyn a long time before he finally came out and met with Mom and me. He was somber when he told us he wanted to call for an ambulance to take Cheralyn across the street to Baptist Hospital. An ambulance? But our car is right outside! I'll carry her. I have before! Why do we need an ambulance? Mother patted me on the hand (like she still does today whenever I get excited or panicked). She nodded at me and I understood her to mean, "It's okay. I'm a nurse and this is how things work." So we waited and followed the ambulance over.

At the hospital, technicians spent most of the day poking her with needles, taking blood, starting IVs, asking questions. I kept eating vending machine food and asking Mom, "When are we going to know anything?" She would just pat my hand (and eat some of my stale food). Mike had come in earlier and we told him all we knew. He took some of my food and then went to pick up Doris. Finally, the test results were in. Mom and I heard one ominous word: leukemia.

Cheralyn stayed in the hospital that night. And the next . . . She seemed to get stronger at first. She would sit up, eat Jell-O. Her color seemed to come back. She and I would watch TV, and I would paint her fingernails. We tried to act normal, thinking that this would pass and we'd all go home when she was strong enough. We didn't tell her right away what the doctors had told us; she was just too tired, too sleepy.

"Am I Going to Die?"

On Sunday, two days later, the doctor came in and explained as best as he could to a fifteen-year-old about leukemia and how it works and how they would be fighting it. Her expression wasn't much different than the time she found out she hadn't gotten the part of Ado Annie in *Oklahoma!*—set, determined, soaking it all in.

Then she nodded, as if to say, "I understand." She boldly asked the doctor, "Am I going to die?"

The doctor was honest and said, "Right now there is a greater chance that you will."

With Cheralyn's battle with leukemia, we had several days that we could have said good-bye, but no one dared. Except Cheralyn. She had missed her good-byes after *Oklahoma!* She was doing this now.

Mother was sitting on one side of her; I was on the other. Michael was at her head, stroking her hair, when Cheralyn took a deep breath, looked at Michael and then at me, and said, "Well, if I wake up with you in the morning, that's okay. And if I wake up with Sis—Charlotta—that's okay too."

Mother didn't go to work at all that week. Or the next. She and Mike, who lived only twenty miles away, took turns staying with

Cheralyn around the clock. (Sometimes we could even get Mother to step into the hospital cafeteria with us for a quick bite to eat.) I missed as many days at school as I could. It was early May, so I did show up to take a test or two so I would at least pass.

Since losing Charlotta, I'd grown more attached to Cheralyn, and I intended to give her every ounce of energy and hope I had. Sometimes I'd lie in bed with her and watch TV. I would read all the cards to her (and there were scores), and she'd tell me where she wanted them taped to the wall. Sometimes I'd help her wash her hair and comb it just right.

After about two weeks in the hospital, two weeks of not getting much better, Cheralyn took a turn for the worse, and the doctors frantically searched for a bone marrow donor. We were ecstatic that Mike was a "perfect" match. The oncologist said that genetically Cheralyn and Mike were nearly as identical as twins, though Mike was more than ten years older. Boy was Mike excited. I remember him, with tears in his eyes, telling the doctor, "You can take both my legs, any major organ—my life—if it will save Cheralyn's life." Though the procedure was expected to be very painful, he was thrilled to know he was going to be a part of Cheralyn's cure.

The bone marrow extraction was ordered for Monday afternoon. Mike was not supposed to eat or drink anything all day. They would draw the marrow from his hip and harvest the sample that would be given to Cheralyn. If it all worked, her body would start producing healthy new blood cells. It all sounded so amazing. She just needed to stabilize long enough for the doctors to feel confident about putting her through the procedure.

Waiting for her to "stabilize," I tried to make her laugh. Sometimes I would walk behind the nurses when they would come into the room and mimic their every move—anything to bring a smile to her sullen face. I would impersonate her favorite teachers, going on and on as I told her all about the homework she was missing. I figured homework was a good enough reason to want to fight to stay alive. Cheralyn was conscientious like that.

One day I let Mike talk me into hiding Cheralyn's French poodle, Tippy, in a suitcase so we could sneak the dog into her hospital room. We figured we could hide her in all the flowers that nearly filled the small room and no one would find out for days. But a nurse heard the bark and "suggested" we get that dog out right away. Cheralyn didn't smile much those days in the hospital, and when she did, it was more of a pained expression. But for Tippy, she laughed. And we realized just how much we all needed that.

It was late Sunday night when I kissed Cheralyn good night. I didn't dare to say good-bye. I'd already said a few too many in my short life. Besides, there was that bone marrow transplant scheduled for Monday, so there was hope.

I remember pulling the door closed quietly and catching one last glimpse of Cheralyn's eyes as Mother settled in the chair next to her bed. Mom opened the Bible and began to read the same verses that Cheralyn loved to hear again and again:

"Therefore we do not lose heart. Though outwardly we are wasting away, yet inwardly we are being renewed day by day.... So we fix our eyes not on what is seen, but what is unseen. For what is seen is temporary, but what is unseen is eternal" (2 Corinthians 4:16–18).

And on Monday morning, at 7:10, Cheralyn woke with Sis.

Talk about bad timing.

The Day Laughter Slipped Away

Cheralyn slipped away from us, and there was nothing we could do about it.

Something else slipped away from me that day too: laughter. It had let me down.

Laughter had not done "good like a medicine" for Cheralyn. I could not hear it anymore. Neither did I want to. The grief was too dark, too loud. Sometimes grief rings so loudly in your ears that you just can't hear anything else. And now the laughter hurt. I could not believe that I would ever laugh again—not like before.

I sat in one of those wooden funeral home chairs. Usually the smell of freshly turned dirt would evoke memories of helping Papaw dig potatoes on the farm. But on this day, May 17, the cemetery dirt nearly made me nauseous. It was the smell of death to me, as we buried Cheralyn alongside Charlotta. Only eighteen months separated their deaths. Hardly enough time for grass to have grown on Charlotta's grave. Hardly enough time to let go of Charlotta, and now we were here again, saying good-bye to Cheralyn.

As the pallbearers lowered her coffin into the ground, I felt this incredible urge to yell, "Stop! Rewind! Let's start all over, God. Your timing stinks. Let's try this again. Take it from the top and let's end this scene a little differently." (I've always had a flair for the dramatic!) By now I was convinced that death, whether it came with or without warning, was one gigantic example of bad timing.

As some men in green shirts threw shovelfuls of dirt onto the lowered casket, I looked at mother and said very deliberately, "Good grief. We're dropping like flies!" We both laughed, but it hurt— like trying to breathe with broken ribs.

That attempt of graveside humor was sheer self-defense. I don't need a professional to tell me that. Those chuckles were merely a means for me to vent my anger, frustration, and pain. Mother put her arms around me and forced me close to her chest. She knew just where that laughter had come from and that soon to follow would be a good long (and much needed) cry. You see, I loved both my sisters more than life itself, and I couldn't imagine my life without either of them in it, and I could not imagine ever laughing again. Really laughing—with a childlike joy.

So much time has gone by now that the majority of my life has been spent without my sisters in it. Yet I still feel that incredible sinking feeling whenever I think of those moments sitting there in that funeral home chair—or when I smell freshly turned earth. I have learned to live with it, work around it, move on, plunge through it. (The more verbs the better.) And I have somehow learned, even though I would not have believed it possible at the time, to laugh again. A healthy laugh, from a healthy place.

But it would take some time. And some patience. From God. From Mother. And from a young man named David Pierce.

Four

Raggedy Andy Gets Married

You, O God, tested us; you refined us like silver. . . . we went through
fire and water, but you brought us to a place of abundance.
Psalm 66:10, 12

The timing of my discovery of "the rush and the thrill" of the sound of laughter—the week before Cheralyn got sick—could have come only from God. But how could I ever laugh again? Why would I want to? I decided to go to college and major in drama—the performing arts. Maybe I couldn't laugh myself, but I still desperately wanted to *perform*—to make other people laugh.

With Dad—and his pastoral career—gone, Mom and I struggled financially. We both worked two jobs. Even so, there was no way I could afford college (especially a private Christian college)—until my mother's brother stepped in, signing a check: all expenses paid for my first year at Trevecca Nazarene College, right in Nashville.

Bless him. My uncle Gerald took care of one huge worry, but things were still tight. So during that summer, before I enrolled, Mom and I decided to move from our five-bedroom, three-bath brick home into a one-bedroom studio apartment at a place called Trevecca Towers—a retirement complex located right next to the college. (A friend of a friend got Mom and me clearance to live with the old folks.) Besides needing the money, I think we desperately wanted to put some distance between us and our pain. Mom and I were alone; even Mike and Doris had moved away, to Georgia. We decided that a smaller dining room table and a fresh start would do us good. So we did what we thought we had to do to survive.

Gotta-Go Sale

Such a drastic downscale and move meant sorting through our lives, cleaning out our closets, putting nearly everything we owned up for sale. Mother and I worked all day one Friday, putting price tags on everything. We tried to agree on all the prices, but whoever had the marker usually won out. I'd ask Mom about something that seemed fairly worthless—like a skillet: "Oooh," Mom would say. And then she'd start thinking—or remembering—about all the nice hot meals that skillet had prepared, or how Cheralyn had held it in her tiny hands, but the pan was too heavy for her to hold and dry so she'd have to set it down and buff it dry. "I'd say, ten dollars?"

I'd just nod and write one dollar. And then with something really nice, like the brand-new, never-used electric blanket someone had given Mom and Dad, she would give just a cursory glance and with disinterest say, "Fifty cents, I guess." I'd mark down ten dollars.

There was so much to get rid of: empty canning jars we had collected from our trips to Nanny and Papaw's (we'd always bring back beans, corn, tomatoes, and jellies that Papaw had grown and Nanny had canned), a set of lamps so ugly that I marked them "free" to whomever would take them, two transistor AM radios (FM was still relatively new), old clothes, used books. You name it, we had it. And it had to go.

I look back now and wish someone had told us to slow down. We sold things then for a nickel that I'd pay fifty dollars to have back again: old sand art jars that Cheralyn and I had made at Vacation Bible School and knickknacks that Charlotta had proudly brought home from her college summer mission trip to Switzerland. Don't worry, we saved a few things. I still have Cheralyn's ballet shoes, Charlotta's hand-embroidered "Foxy-Lady" shirt, Cheralyn's favorite pair of blue jeans and Charlotta's favorite devotional book. Yard sale material for sure, but to me, they are priceless.

Saturday morning we got up early and put the posters on trees and light poles near the house. I had painted some posters the night before that read Gotta-Go Sale! (I wanted to write Name It, Claim

It, Take It Sale but there wasn't enough room on the poster.) And then I went back to the dressing room (bathroom) and put on my face—my clown face. Literally. The entire day I dressed like Raggedy Andy, complete with red yarn hair, white face paint, round red cheeks, navy blue knickers, a giant bow tie, and a black triangle nose.

That Raggedy Andy costume—it was the mask I counted on to get me through one horrible day of my life. I would stand at the edge of the street, like someone in the big city hailing a cab. "Everything's going!" I'd shout from time to time. "Going, going, gone!" Once in a while I'd do a cartwheel, and Mother would just laugh and shake her head. Occasionally I would stop and survey what was left of our belongings, assess the damage, but before any of the war zone pictures could sink into my brain, another car would approach and I was back in the circus.

When the sale had ended, Mom and I had saved a few pans and dishes for our new kitchen and Charlotta's piano—we couldn't sell that. (I think Mom wanted me to mark it at one million dollars; I priced it at ten million.)

David Pierce came over late that afternoon and helped me, Mom, my aunt Ruth (Mom's sister), and her husband move the piano and a few remaining boxes onto the back of his pickup truck. By time he drove up, I'd taken off my Raggedy Andy suit. Just as well. I wasn't exactly stunning in a clown face.

Hiding Behind the Mask

What *was* I doing that day? Some people call it the "game face." Some call it avoidance. Years later a Christian counselor called my clown suit my own form of dissociation. She proposed that dissociation is sometimes a sweet gift from God.

Huh?! She explained how it works: "You have just gone through a painful trauma. Perhaps you are aware of what is going on around you, but you feel as if you are watching yourself—your own life—from the sidelines." She used the phrase "semi-out-of-body experience."

I quipped, "You mean my 'out-to-lunch' experience?"

She smiled. She knew about my penchant for humor—the good of it, and the bad of it. You see, Alison Evans, my Christian counselor, went to college with me. While I studied acting, she studied me! She knew Chonda Courtney, the drama student, the actress. Oh, I'd taken off the physical Raggedy Andy costume but I was still play-acting, hiding behind a mask. It was made of distrust and its "face" reflected sarcasm and forced humor. Here I was, learning how to make people laugh, but in self-protection I was forgetting nearly everything I had ever learned as a child about healthy laughter and hearty guffaws, like the time mother's Jell-O salad hit the ceiling of our Chevy one night on the way to church. (Dad had tried to miss the bump—he said.) That kind of laugh was filled with pure joy—even if Mom didn't laugh while she scraped peaches and cottage cheese off the ceiling of the car.

Throughout my college years—and even beyond—my laughter came from a heart filled with pain—bitter, cutting humor that reeked with unhealthy sarcasm. One of my mother's favorite reprimands to me was a loving, "Watch your smart-mouth attitude, young lady!" You get the picture?

But why should I "watch my attitude"? I wondered. I was alone, and I believed I was going to stay that way—that suited me fine. Mike had moved away. Dad had left. Charlotta and Cheralyn had gone to heaven. And Mom was trying to teach me to be civil—when I preferred to be on my own deserted island! I thought that I should be able to come and go as I pleased, say what I wanted, see whom I wanted, and *not* see whom I wanted. I felt I should be allowed to decide who stepped onto my island and who didn't. And when I was with my friends, I may as well have just stepped through the slit in the sheet and said, with a giant smile, "Welcome to my show, everyone!" No one was going to get close to me no matter what excuse he or she used.

My Own Little Island

I was in charge, and I was in control. And if I wanted to see someone, like David Pierce, then I would decide that. During our senior year in high school, I had signed up to take guitar lessons from him (even though he had only started playing himself, and he didn't give guitar lessons). That summer after I had graduated, I went to where he worked almost every afternoon for weeks. (It takes a while to learn the G, C, and D chords.) He had one of those jobs where he didn't have a lot to do: he worked at the water plant and every so often he'd just throw a few scoops of chemicals in some tanks and say, "There, that should be safe enough to drink." And then we'd play guitars.

Maybe I was attracted to David because he had known Cheralyn so well. (It certainly wasn't his guitar playing!) In the last few months of Cheralyn's life, we had all shared some wonderful times sledding down the hill in the snow, sneaking out of sixth period at school to get an IcEE, and practicing pirouettes in my living room. At any rate, I liked being with David. He had become my best friend, and he always made me laugh. I was comfortable being around him—and that was enough for now.

One Sunday evening, shortly after my high school graduation, David and I were having a friendly conversation on the steps of the church, a church that had been busy with two funerals and a wedding in the last eighteen months. Usually we had no trouble talking about any and everything. But today he stared at the ground and kept his hands busy by breaking a twig into tiny pieces. He had said that he needed to talk with me and then he just clammed up. (Men!) "Are you okay?" I asked, recognizing that his behavior was unlike my outgoing, talkative friend. "Yeah, sure. I'm fine."

We repeated this two or three more times before he finally looked up from the ground, his head tilted slightly. He squinted as if he were looking directly into the sunlight. "It's just ... it's just that I think I've fallen in love with you."

I should have been excited. I should have hugged his neck and said, "Me too, baby!" After all, that's what I had been thinking—at the prom, at the "guitar lessons." But in my head I could hear the tires screech to a halt. I braced myself and looked away from his squinty expression. I smiled (oh, I was smiling big, the same big stage smile I'd flashed only a few weeks before in *Oklahoma!*) and said, "Wow, Mr. Cheatham County High School [the big award he had just gotten the week before at school] is in love with *me*?" Then I looked at him—because this was the important part—and said, "Gee, thanks."

I exited the scene (almost sprinting) and went back into the church, leaving him there on the steps, breaking twigs and squinting at nothing. Whew! That was close, but for now my little island was safe.

I quickly learned the art of self-protection. In some ways it's like wearing a permanent costume or mask. It's all about being on guard against the next hurt around the corner. Never allowing anyone to step within your circle, taking for granted that he would hurt you anytime, any moment, for any reason.

I wore the mask of sarcasm and at-arm's-length humor—for years—because I didn't trust anyone. Just a tad too much grief for one person to handle, I thought. And perhaps that is largely true. Maybe I thought I had to control my emotions to feel as if I had some control over when and how I let myself be hurt. Evelyn Minshull must know what I'm talking about. She said it so much more eloquently than I can in her article "Shall We Pretend?" (*Today's Christian Woman*, July/August 1984): "Facades protect us from the embarrassment of 'breaking apart,' of being totally vulnerable, dependent, stripped of all defense and dignity, in the presence of others." Assuming pain was just around the corner, I lived my life waiting for it. Looking for it. On guard against it.

At Trevecca I stayed on guard by staying busy. I ran for freshman class vice-president and won. (I thought about running for president, but it sounded like too much responsibility. Vice-president was a lot more fun!) I worked at the switchboard and learned the names of everyone on campus before I learned their faces. On weekends I worked at the nursing home with Mother. David, who had not left my circle of friends, went to a university about thirty miles away, and sometimes he would come up and watch a basketball game with me or see a play I was a part of. (*The Music Man*, remember?)

Toward the end of my first year of college, I left the dorm (two blocks away) and moved back into the apartment with Mom. One afternoon she glanced up from a book and asked, "Guess who is transferring to Trevecca this fall?" I didn't have a guess. "David."

"Great! We'll go sledding in the winter. We'll play guitars late at night by the fountain on campus. We'll raid the refrigerator at Mom's while we're studying. It will be like old times! Only without that mushy stuff. I hope he's gotten that out of his system," I quipped to Mother.

Besides, I was now dating someone else. But when David arrived on campus, he was not so much a comforting, familiar face, as a reminder of things I didn't want to think about. And he was always around. Even around the apartment. I would go out on dates, stay out late, and come home to find David eating my food, at my table, talking and laughing with my mother! And not just once or twice, but every day. It seems he had gotten a job in the maintenance department of our apartment building. At lunch time he would just make himself at home. At supper he would just make himself at home. And Mother didn't help much: at Christmas time she hung a stocking with his name on it. She would even introduce us to strangers as her kids. (Plural!)

One day, as he helped himself to our bologna, he asked me, "Are you still dating that goofy guy?" He looked up from his sandwich, sporting just a little mayonnaise in the corner of his mouth.

I snapped back, "Yeah, as a matter of fact, I think he's a cousin to that weird girl you've been going out with lately."

I knew this was going to be a long year!

Life of the Party

By the end of the year it was obvious to me that Trevecca wasn't working out. (Too crowded.) Many of my classmates were old friends from South Carolina—friends who had grown up with Cheralyn, Charlotta, and me. Seeing them—and David—every day made me miss my sisters. Besides, I wanted more experience as a theater arts major, and Trevecca wasn't the place to be. (At least that's what I told Mother.) So I transferred to Austin Peay State University my third year, about forty miles away. There I would find new faces and forget about the old ones.

A whole new world opened up for me at this university, more opportunities and not all of them good. The theater department was known for their quality productions and speech classes. The head of the department, Dr. Fillipo, became a great friend and advisor. He saw that I gained all the experience I could in those few short years, from managing the box office to building sets, from stage hand to leading lady.

There I found a new mask, one that allowed me to become the life of the party. Unfortunately, as at most secular universities, there was a party on every corner. And many of the choices I made raked against every standard ever set for me in a Christian home. Before long I became weary of the mask and could not remember what I looked like beneath the paints. I knew I was away from God, and I was getting tired of my one-woman show.

The Awakening

One morning, while walking to class, I noticed a young couple standing on some steps, engaged in a heavy conversation. Tears were streaming down the girl's face, and the boy brushed a finger underneath her falling tears as if trying to catch them before they hit the ground. He tenderly stroked the hair from her face, and they embraced. As I walked to the other side and headed toward my classroom, I noticed his face leaning across her shoulder. I waited skeptically for his expression behind her back. I just knew he was probably grinning, peeking at his watch before he would move on. But what I noticed were his eyes: They were squeezed shut, and his face was soaked with his own tears.

Could it be that once in awhile someone really does reach out and hold you, accept you as you are? The funny stuff? The painful stuff? I stood there ages, but they never noticed me. And that's when I knew. . . .

I immediately turned around, walked down the steps and off the campus. I got into my car and headed to Nashville as fast as I could. I drove forty-two miles straight home, too fast! It was as if I had had a major revelation in my heart and had to tell David. I wanted to throw my arms around his neck and say, "I'm here! I'm here!"

I found him working in the basement shop at the apartment complex. He was rebuilding a carburetor for his car. His shirt was sweaty, and his hands were greasy (perhaps I wouldn't throw my arms around his neck). I asked him what he was doing and he explained, "The car doesn't run smoothly. You see, if there is too much gas and not enough air coming into the barrel, the car'll choke out and sputter and spit and eventually die." (Actually, that was a little more explanation than I was looking for!) He went on: "Or if there is too much air and not enough gas, it'll wheeze, sputter, and spit and eventually die. I'm trying to find just that right balance where everything will run smoothly."

Find the balance and live! Right? I wanted to interject. Yes, yes— we were on the same wavelength, I could tell. I took a deep breath and tried to explain to him how I felt, how I had always had this special attachment for him, how I always believed he was more special than any of the guys I had dated since he had known me (five, six, maybe seven—I'm not sure). I told him I loved him—that I was tired of our relationship sputtering and dying.

Silence. He was squinting again, thinking. And in a slow, broken speech he admitted that he loved me too—in his own special way.

Special way? I'd heard that line before. (I think I had even said it.)

By now, David had learned a few more chords on the guitar and he went home that night and wrote a song for me that he played the next day: "I Love You in My Own Special Way." He sang the song, and when he had finished, it was pretty clear to me that he thought of me like a sister. Our carburetor was sputtering badly.

Getting Away

Now I really had to get away. I went all the way to Cynthiana, Kentucky, which is about twenty miles west of Lexington because my cousin, Brad Whalen, and his friend, Steve Whitaker, played guitars in this restaurant, and they needed a keyboard player. It was summertime. Why not me? Why not go? So I packed up my things, said good-bye to Mom, and headed north.

That summer David wrote me letters, telling me how life was going back in Tennessee. He'd tell me about Mom, what he had been eating (at my house), and how his school was going. And in his letters I could hear his voice, and I missed him. I was lonely there in Cynthiana (and the country music wasn't helping much either!).

When Brad asked me to play in his wedding that summer, I reached out again and invited David to come and accompany me on his guitar. (There were lots of pretty songs he could play with only three chords.) We had a great day together. Love was in the air! After the reception, I took David back to Uncle Gerald's and noticed that David was having trouble talking. (I recognized what this meant! I had seen that almost six years before!) He asked me if I wanted to walk. I took his hand, and we walked along the giant backyard until we came to a footbridge that led over a small creek. We sat on the bridge. My heart was pounding and in my mind I was practicing saying, "Yes, yes, I'll marry you!" This was going to be the sweetest moment of my life.

David stumbled around with his words. He searched about, probably for a twig to play with while he thought. "Chonda . . . ah, listen . . . I was wondering if . . . ah . . ."

"Yes! I mean—yes?"

"I've been doing a lot of thinking since you moved away. I've really missed you. You might have been able to tell that in the letters."

And?

"And here is what I was wondering."

Yes?

"Chonda, you wanna go steady with me?"

I laughed—one of those kind of laughs I usually give when I'm confused and I need some time to sort things out. I thought, *Steady? What is wrong with this guy! We've known each other for years. He loves me, and I love him. And he asks me to go steady with him like some high school couple?* I wanted the fireworks, the theme music, the big production. But David didn't see our relationship like that. He genuinely wanted to go steady—to court me and to truly get to know me. And after all, he did know the intricacies of the carburetor.

Coming Home to Stay

I moved back to Tennessee at the end of the summer and returned to APSU. This time I decided to live with my cousins on their nearby farm. It saved me money, and Mother didn't worry about me getting into trouble as much with Jerry and Ann to watch over me.

The first major production that year was a musical called *A Little Night Music*. One of the most beautiful solos in the production is the song "Send in the Clowns." Each night as the music would swell and the lights would shift, the lyrics rolled around my head. It's a song about timing and how it seems to be all wrong. I couldn't help but think of David: *"Me, here at last on the ground—you in midair."* It kept happening to David and me; were we ever going to get it *right?* So we didn't have to "send in the clowns"?

David came to our final performance. After the play, he drove me home and wanted to know if I'd like to take a walk. It was late and cold but David's walks usually meant something was on his mind. (He had begun to squint already.) I had noticed the nervousness on the ride home—sweaty palms, fragmented sentences. I decided maybe he needed to borrow some money! But suddenly, under the giant oak in the front yard, he blurted out, "Okay, I love ya—wantcha to be my wife."

I laughed. I told him not to joke like that. But the look in his eyes (it was that familiar squint) and the way he held my hands let me know that he was serious. He was not pretending; this was it. And as he lifted his hand toward my face, he caught my teardrop just before it hit the ground, and I knew I could trust him.

I admit—to this day I struggle with allowing myself to get close enough to people to truly trust them with the real me. And sometimes the sarcasm slips in. (I'm not naturally funny; but I am naturally sarcastic. I think some churches call it the carnal nature of man. That's what Mother calls it anyway!) People who know me well realize that this "humor violation" stems from a pocket of pain. They grin and begin to pray. (Especially, my mother.)

One of the most timely turning points for healing in my life was allowing myself to trust David—trust him enough to marry him. Together we continue to work to find the proper balance, for only then can our relationship run smoothly (as smoothly as his old Oldsmobile with the rebuilt carburetor).

On that special night, David and I knelt together under the oak tree and asked God for his direction in our lives as well as thanking him for his faithful timing that allowed us—as awkward as it seemed—to grow toward each other rather than away from each other.

I remember a critical conversation I had with Alison, my girlfriend from college, who is now a skilled psychologist and still my best friend. I visit her as a friend—but capitalize on the free therapy! I think it works out great: I learn about my psyche, id, superego. . . and she gets lots of free videos and books!

One day we talked about that yard sale and my Raggedy Andy getup. That's when she said that masks can have their value. When Abraham's wife, Sarah, found out that she was to have a son (and she was at an age much older than my own mother is right now), she "laughed to herself" (Genesis 18:12). It is easy to see how this may have been a disbelieving laugh, a sarcastic laugh. And maybe Sarah used this laugh to defend herself against disappointment. But God did not seem pleased with her attitude: "The LORD said to Abraham, 'Why did Sarah laugh and say, "Will I really have a child, now that I am old?"' . . . Sarah was afraid, so she lied and said, 'I did not laugh.' But he said, 'Yes, you did laugh'" (Genesis 18:13–15).

Obviously, the place where Sarah was—disbelieving laughter, sarcastic laughter, a laughter that hid her true pain—was not the place God really wanted her to be. (And after all, she was dealing with God, not with humans, who can disappoint one another.)

God allowed me protection behind a mask for a season; yet I don't believe that God was happy with my attempting to keep everyone around me, including him, at arm's length.

"The real trick," said Alison, "is to move back into life, into society after the trauma, perhaps with some scars, but without the mask. And that's what God has equipped me to help you do—take the clown suit off and leave it off." Send away the clowns.

Hear it from Evelyn Minshull as well, as she continued to write about our self-protection and how it may prevent us from finding help: "While the facade offers genuine elements of protection—guarding our emotional wounds, just as gauze and ointment promote healing for physical laceration—it also bars us from receiving other helps, which we may require."

As for Alison, she and I kept talking about the most obvious and visible representation of my wound: the day I dressed up as a clown. I asked what I thought was a hard question: "So, where was God during our yard sale? Did he even care that we were losing everything? That every memento that represented twenty-five years of marriage and the lives of two beautiful girls had dwindled down to no more than could be contained in one egg carton box? Where was God then?"

Alison confidently offered her "help": "He was in the middle of the street with a teenager who was dressed like Raggedy Andy and waving cars into the drive, getting her safely through the day."

I had never considered my Raggedy Andy experience to be something God had been a part of. It took a while for me to understand that he was there—that day and throughout the subsequent difficult days of "my youth" (oh, I'm sounding almost middle-aged). But God had been with me when Mom and I had sold nearly everything we owned for pennies. He was there with me when I put on the grease paint and again when I took it off. He was there on that old bridge when David asked me to go steady with him and under the oak when he asked me to marry him.

And he was there the following spring, when David and I were married, outdoors at my cousins' farm. I had always dreamed that on my wedding day I would ride off in a horse-drawn carriage. I had made a few phone calls and believed that was what we were getting. But when David helped me up into the wagon (not carriage), we both noticed immediately that, instead of horses, two gray mules clip-clopped along the gravel road, kicking up dust. We just got comfortable and rode along—smiling and waving and *laughing*.

Five

Radioactive Tomatoes

Here I have lamely related to you the uneventful chronicle of two foolish
children in a flat who most unwisely sacrificed for each other the greatest
treasures of their house. But in a last word to the wise of these days let it be
said that of all who give gifts these two were the wisest.
"The Gift of the Magi," O. Henry

I remember after Cheralyn died, Mother and I enrolled in a ceramics class, all materials supplied. I was the youngest one in there. (Even twenty years later, I would probably still be the youngest one in there.) Once a week, Mom and I worked side by side, pushing, squeezing, molding, shaping, painting, and finally glazing our finished products. Mom made a fruit bowl (not much skill in that, I thought). And I made a gravy bowl—with a lid and a little notch in the side for the spoon. We would set these on the table whenever anyone would come over and hope someone would ask about them.

"And where did you get these?" someone would say and point to our collection.

"Ahh, those simple dishes?" I'd say. Then I would ruminate momentarily, as if searching my memory, and explain, "We made those."

"Made them?"

"Yes, of course, first we took the clay ..." And before that person could protest, I was off on my guided tour through ceramic production. The bowl and dish were simple glass dishes (at least Mom's was anyway). I'm sure sometimes people just wanted the short version (if they wanted any version at all). But there was no way I could explain how I was handed a lump (a neat little square) of clay and how

I pounded, punched, cut, and culled out a form, then detailed it with what looked like tiny flowers and lastly created a glossy finish with the glaze and a hot kiln. There was no short version to this story. (Apologies to my former guests.)

Now if I tell you that I eventually came to turn from grief and anger and sarcastic, bitter humor to a joyful laughter, you may ask how. Believe me, there is no short version. But as with the little gravy bowl, there was a lot of time involved. I could not shape and then glaze on the same day. There were steps to take. One I've already told you about—when Minnie Pearl stopped me short with these words: "You gotta love people to make 'em want to laugh. . . . You really won't know anything about laughing until you have found peace with God and love him first." I took another step with the help of my husband, David. Many times he has demonstrated to me the kind of sacrificial giving that is the hallmark of a loving God.

All We Had Was Each Other

Soon after David and I were married I became pregnant (surprise!), and Chera Kay was born in the winter of 1984. When she was an infant, we were living in a small apartment at a motel. Yes, a motel! David was the on-site maintenance man, and in the winter months, while Opryland was closed, I was a desk clerk. We had a great setup! The owners of the motel were like parents to us: they housed us, fed us, and when I was sick, they sent housekeeping down to run the vacuum and make the beds. We hated to leave them (and give up the little bathroom soaps). But David had an English degree and was tired of being a maintenance man. He had been offered a training position as a Nursing Home Administrator. (I know, it wasn't exactly "in his field," but at the time, this sounded like a good opportunity. We were just trying to find our niche.) So we packed up and moved to Glasgow, Kentucky.

We borrowed some money from the bank and bought David three suits, some shirts, and a couple of ties that he could mix and match and make it appear as if he had six different outfits. With our meager savings (all $327.46!) we found a little rental house in great need of repair (but at least it had air conditioning) and moved in. We had no stove or washing machine. We had one hot plate and a toaster oven. (Thank heaven for wedding gifts!) And we bought a refrigerator for fifty dollars. We ate macaroni and cheese just about every night. (I know, I know this sounds cliché, but David did insist on Beanie Weenies for Friday nights and hot dogs for Sunday dinner.) David's paycheck barely covered the rent, the car payment, and the suit payment, leaving a few dollars left over for groceries. Here we were in a "new world" to us and with no Pampers, no television, no phone, and no friends. All we had was each other.

And our tomatoes—we grew tomatoes. I'm positive those homegrown fruits saved our lives. We planted them at the corner of the house, right beneath the drip from the air conditioner condensation drain. At first we thought maybe the dripping water had some positively charged ions or something, because the plants grew up past the windows, up to the gutters and actually lay on the roof of the house! Later, our neighbor asked us why we planted the climbing vines instead of the bush plants. I think David told him something about a NASA experiment he was involved in.

Too bad we couldn't have grown Pampers. We had six cloth diapers that I was constantly washing out and hanging on the line to dry. If it was a rainy day, Chera Kay would wear dish towels until the diapers could dry in front of the fan. Some may think the sight of a baby crawling around with the pictures of pots and pans on her fanny is cute, but it wasn't easy trying to remember which tea towels were real tea towels and which ones were diapers. The three of us would take long walks together (once the real diapers dried, of course), sit on the back porch for hours singing and playing the guitar, laugh at the cute things Chera Kay would do, or tie more twine to the tomato plants.

My mom and stepfather, Sam, drove up from Nashville just to bring us a television set. It was one of those cabinet models with a turntable and an AM/FM stereo and fancy cloth-covered hi-fi speakers mounted in each end. (I hadn't seen one like this since I was a little girl.) The television was black-and-white and the reception had

this washed-out look, sort of like an x-ray—but the sound was great!
We had cleared out a spot against the far wall (it took up the whole
wall) and I made some popcorn on the hot plate (popcorn was
cheap).

After Mom had gone back home, David and I sliced some
tomatoes and prepared to watch our first evening of television in
weeks.

I didn't think the picture was too washed out. And if you con-
centrated on one spot, the constant flipping of the vertical hold
was not too distracting either, but David couldn't enjoy the show.
So he took some of his old maintenance man tools, slid the cabinet out from the wall and crawled in behind the set. The last thing
I remember him calling out to me was, "Tell me when this looks
better!" Seconds later, there came two popping sounds: the first
one came from somewhere inside the television, the other when
David jumped back and hit his head on the wall. The TV screen
washed out bright like a camera flash. Then the picture folded
down to a thin, skinny line before shrinking to a pinpoint of light
that seemed to hang right in the center of the dark green screen
for days. Gray smoke puffed up from behind the set, and I heard
David say, "Uh-oh."

"Oh, that's a lot better," I announced, suddenly losing my
appetite for popcorn. That was the night our television set became
a coffee table.

The Gift

A few weeks after that, David came home for lunch and said
my brother Mike had called him at work. I was to call him back. So
that afternoon I carried Chera on my hip and walked to a nearby
convenience store to use the pay phone. Mike and Doris, who lived
in Mt. Vernon, Ohio, wanted to see the baby and suggested that we
meet them in Cincinnati for the weekend.

Mike said, "We can split a hotel room, eat out, and play golf
the next day on a new course I've been wanting to try out. Doris is
dying to see the baby. How about it?"

It sounded wonderful. But, well, "We really couldn't afford it right now. . . ."

As big brothers sometimes do, he said, "Oh, come on. We'll take care of the weekend."

We went back and forth a few times and finally I burst into tears. "Look, we just can't do it. We don't have gas money to make the three-hour drive. Chera Kay is wearing dish towels. I'm nursing her four times a day and refueling with macaroni and cheese and radioactive tomatoes. We're doing our best to keep our heads above water. Furthermore, if we had the money to golf, we would use it to buy diapers. So the answer is NO."

Mike grew horribly silent.

Then that tone that sometimes parents take with their children—the one where concern and I'm-gonna-whoop-you-good mingle—came out as he said, "If you had just told me earlier, I'd have sent you some money!"

I knew he would. But David and I were both pretty independent. We wouldn't admit even to each other—much less to someone else—that we were both miserable! I had hated leaving Nashville, my mother, and the upcoming season at Opryland. And as for David, well, nursing home administrator trainee wasn't exactly the future he'd hoped for.

Mike ended the conversation by telling me to walk to Western Union, because he was going to wire me some money.

When David returned for the evening, I had the table set and had sliced some tomatoes and made a pot roast for supper. I was so excited with the anticipation of giving him the news of our impending trip to Cincinnati. David loves to golf, and it had been months and months since he could afford even to play Putt-Putt. So when he came in the door, I had Chera Kay dressed in her Sunday bonnet and our suitcase packed so that we could leave after supper. I yelled, "Surprise! Guess what you get to do this weekend!!!??"

David just stood there, dumbfounded. So I started blurting out our fun news: "Mike sent us some money, and we're going to eat out and stay in a motel and you and Mike are going to golf all day!

And Doris is going to take Chera and me to pick out some baby clothes. Isn't that great!?!?"

David slipped into his chair at the dinner table, the blood drained from his face, causing the tomatoes to look that much brighter. "I can't play golf," he said.

"Sure you can. I know it's been awhile. And maybe you'll hook or slice or whatever, but it'll all come back to you."

"No. I mean I can't play because . . ." He began to pull some money out of his pocket, " . . . because I pawned my golf clubs today." On the table he laid out some new, folded bills: Pampers and food money.

Thirty dollars. That's what he'd gotten for the clubs. He could have played with them for years to come—could have enjoyed hour upon hour of hitting that little white ball all over the pasture. He read about golf, talked it, slept it—he even watched it on TV! But he cashed them in for two weeks worth of Pampers, more macaroni and cheese, and some Beanie Weenies.

There are moments in a marriage, I've learned, where couples can grow apart, but I've also discovered that husband and wife can grow together. I remember on Papaw's farm a pair of twisted trees that grew through an old fence. They were wrapped one around the other. At some places along the twisted trunks the fence was wedged between the barks; at other places the trunks were so meshed that I could not discern where one trunk stopped and the other began. At those points, they were as one. That was what that moment was like for us. As the money lay on the table and David was saying, "Go get the Pampers," we grew together; there was no way to tell where he ended and I began.

Leaning on the Lord

To this day I have an incredible respect for David Pierce. God brought him into my life and orchestrated our relationship. David doesn't use the word *adversity*. What some may think as an impossible situation, he shrugs his shoulders and says, "Okay, what are our options?" He gathers strength for the day and plows through. And he laughs.

Do you know what he did when I told him Mike had sent us money—he hadn't needed to pawn the golf clubs? He laughed. *We* laughed.

I can't say we stayed in Kentucky very long. Within six months of our arrival, we had a big yard sale and sold what wasn't in the pawn shop. (David took thirty bucks and got his golf clubs back.) We used the rest of the money to move back to Nashville. (We sold the giant coffee table for five dollars and tomatoes for ten cents each. And neither of us dressed like a clown.)

Looking back now, those were some of the sweetest days in our marriage. And even though we were lonely, broke, and scared—just where the Lord needed us to be—we would talk to one another for hours. And you can't help but learn about one another when you do that. We discovered so much about ourselves, about loving and trusting one another, and supporting one another even in the tough times. No, David did not become a nursing home administrator. So was it wasted time? Did God play a trick on us? I don't think so. You see, we learned what it was like to truly lean on the Lord for daily bread! We discovered together that he is a trustworthy God. He will not leave us or forsake us in the days of plenty or in the tough days. Miss Minnie had said something about finding peace with God. The evidence of sweet peace came for David and me as we learned to trust God in all things and to trust the incredible love he has blessed us with.

And besides learning to trust one another, we learned other things too: 143 recipes with macaroni and cheese and knowing that even in the poorest of days we could find something to laugh about. We also learned that anyone can really do without golf! And Pampers! And a TV! And a stove! That you can grill, slice, roll, cube, fry, and boil bologna, and you've still got bologna. But whatever you do, grow tomatoes (right next to your air conditioner). They could save your life!

Six

Time for Popcorn

God can heal a broken heart, when he is given all the pieces.
Anonymous

I don't even really remember her name; I think it was Elizabeth. She was an attractive woman, dark hair, in her forties probably. I remembered seeing her in the audience earlier, smiling and laughing (I always appreciate it when people do that). I'd told my story—the funny stuff, the painful losses, how I'd eventually found my way to the grin after the grim and was coming off the platform when she stopped me on the last step.

"Can I talk to you for a moment?" What I saw in her eyes halted me. They were deep-set, surrounded by laugh lines. There was a sparkle there, the kind of sparkle any comedian can appreciate. Yet just beneath the sparkle was a dark and dull spot that I'd seen before. Her eyes spoke to me even before her voice: "I've seen the same dark valley that you spoke of. Will you listen to my story as well?"

I finished up my good-byes with a few people standing around. As we stood together at the front of the stage, she told me her story, one that happened over ten years ago. As I remember it . . .

She'd had three boys. Stairsteps. I think the oldest was eight. She and her husband—busy parents—were active in their local church. A good marriage. Happy family. Her husband loved to fish. He loved to take the boys to a nearby lake. They had a favorite fishing hole where they all enjoyed themselves.

Then on one particular day, on the lakeshore the boys found an old dilapidated raft tied to a tree. They begged their father to let them row out into the middle of the lake on this raft. No, he said.

After a few hours of fishing, their father ran out of bait. He told them to sit still while he walked to the top of the bank to his truck.

When he came back, the boys weren't on the bank. Nor was the raft tied to the tree. His boys were out in the lake, splashing, screaming, floundering frantically in the choppy water. They'd obviously gone out on the raft, and something had gone terribly wrong.

This dad swam as fast as he could and reached his five-year-old. He got his son to a floating piece of the old raft, told him to hold on to it, and then went for the other two boys. The eight-year-old was desperately trying to save his baby brother, but by the time their father could reach the spot, they were silent and gone.

The father, screaming in frustration and pain, couldn't reach them. Then, when he swam back to his younger son, the piece of wood was empty. All three boys were dead.

She stopped at that point of her story. We stood there silently. Waiting as if to catch our breath. I didn't know what I was *supposed* to do after such a story. When *I* tell a few stories, people sometimes laugh, sometimes cry. This story stopped me cold. I leaned toward the edge of the platform and stumbled back against the steps. I could barely stand up. Then regaining my balance, I stepped toward her, threw my arms around her, and we cried together.

"How did you make it through that?" I asked. "How in the world do you keep going? How were you ever able to smile again, much less laugh again?"

She said something that we've all heard before: "It takes time. Time does heal things a bit."

We talked for a while about finding counselors and praying for one another. Before long we were chatting rather light-heartedly, and after a while we were chuckling about something we'd heard on the radio. How does that happen?

Looking at Elizabeth and seeing laugh lines around her eyes, a cheeriness in her voice as she shared a funny joke she'd heard on the radio, seeing her alive, breathing, sane, after all that she'd been through, well, that's when the evidence of something so much bigger than you or me is overpowering. When a sweet and gentle spirit can breeze across sunken shoulders and whisper peace and joy to broken hearts—that's when you must throw up your hands and say, "There is no explanation. It is undeniably God, and in him there is joy and laughter after the rain. After the pain."

Time Does Not Heal All Wounds

What is there about time and its relationship to healing? I think again of my loss of Cheralyn. It has been twenty years since I laid in that hospital bed with Cheralyn and talked about what was going on at school and made plans of what we would do when she would come home. Twenty years, and I can still close my eyes and see her warm smile; I can remember her soft touch and the smell of her hair.

Once in a while I will drive by the cemetery and glance at my sisters' graves. They're now covered with well-rooted grass. All the "little shrubs" are now tall. The weeds keep creeping up across their names and the stones have weathered.

Twenty years. So much time has passed that it is hard to imagine what Cheralyn would look like now. Would she have had children? At times I just ache in my heart, missing her, missing our time together.

I remember hearing that phrase "Time will heal things" so often that I decided that I would never pass that word of wisdom on to any broken-hearted mourner sitting on the family couch in a funeral home. But in recent years, when I find myself searching for the right words for someone grieving, that very sentence has slipped off my tongue.

I've said it, and yet I have learned that "time" itself doesn't heal much of anything. I think that something happened to Elizabeth that she was not able to recognize—or at least articulate to me. I think Benjamin Disraeli was wrong when he said, "Time is the great physician." I say, *time* is not what counts; it's what we allow to happen *during* that passage of time. If we do nothing, then tomatoes will not ripen, popcorn will burn, and wounds will not heal. Let me explain.

I can remember Nanny setting some green tomatoes on the windowsill in the kitchen of her old farmhouse and saying, "Now give that a little time, and they'll turn red and be perfect for eating." Time must pass before the tomatoes will ripen, that's true, but they will not ripen in the closet.

My husband wanted to go back to school. "In two years I can get a master's degree," he said.

"That seems like a long time for reading and writing," I said.

"Two years will pass by anyway," he responded. And you know what? He was right. Two years from now, two years will have passed. Time will pass—it always has, and as long as the Lord tarries it always will. Only this time, when these two years pass, he will have a degree that he didn't have before.

As time passes, we can watch things happen. Fruits ripen and people become educated—providing the fruits are placed in the sunshine and the people go to class.

If we put too much stock in the idea that if only time will hurry up and pass, then everything will be all right, we wind up watching the clock—believing the passing seconds are doing something valuable for us, believing that perhaps even some healing is taking place, simply because the clock is ticking—and we wind up burning the popcorn.

My husband does lots of things well, but cooking is not one of them. Not even the microwave can make him look good. But to his credit, over the years he has taken the trouble to memorize the recipe for microwavable popcorn: put the bag in with THIS SIDE UP facing up, punch three-and-a-half minutes, and serve hot. But not long ago I got a new microwave—one with a light bulb inside so I can watch things cook. My husband took charge of family night by volunteering for popcorn duty. He punched in the time like so many nights before and three-and-a-half minutes later we were opening windows and fanning smoke to outside.

"But that time has always worked before!" he cried, using a pillow to fan away the smoke.

"But you did not check the wattage of the microwave, did you?" I responded.

He shook his head, guilty.

"Nor did you consider the net weight of the pack, the viscosity of the butter, the reflective consistency of the packaging, or even the added heat generated by the single light bulb, did you?"

I was afraid he'd weep if I continued further. But the point is, time is only one factor to be considered.

But don't take my word for it. Look at the New Testament. The Bible often refers to time in the sense of "fullness of time." In the fullness of time, Jesus was born on earth. In the fullness of time, he died. In the fullness of time, he will come again. Another writer, Joseph Allison, says it this way: "Fulfilled time is a time measurement that is based on *conditions* rather than the *calendar.*"

In God's scheme chronological time is not the measure of "fullness" or "ripeness." Think about the popcorn David cooked (burnt). He was assuming that three-and-a-half minutes "on" would do the job right. What he didn't think about was the extra power of this new oven.

Nanny always told us that in time the green tomatoes will turn red, but she always placed them on the sunny window sill—something we should have noticed.

And when David went back to school, he went to class, did the homework, wrote the papers, and took the tests.

So it's not time alone that cooks (or burns), or ripens, or educates, or heals—it's *what goes on during that time.* How much heat is generated? How much sunshine is present? How many courses do you complete? How will you let God minister to your pain? Perhaps, before any more time passes, *you* must embrace God's grace and mercy available for your salvation or for your healing.

Time doesn't heal our spirits. God does—as we give him permission to work in us, through us, and with us.

And that healing can start today.

The Day of God's Favor

Check out this Bible verse. You may have heard it before, but look at it with fresh eyes. It's 2 Corinthians 6:2: "Now is the time of God's favor, now is the day of salvation."

Wherever you are right now—this is the day of God's favor. Wait, there's more. Let me back up and give you 2 Corinthians 6:1 and 2: "As God's fellow workers we urge you not to receive God's grace in vain. For he says, 'In the time of my favor I heard you, and in the day of salvation I helped you.' I tell you, now is the time of God's favor, now is the day of salvation."

God has blessed me with two very down-to-earth pastors. Would you believe it—they're brothers. Allen Jackson and Phillip Jackson. (No, Phillip doesn't coach basketball, and Allen doesn't sing country music!) Last fall Pastor Allen preached an entire series on one word for six weeks. One word. (You'd think we would have been the first in line at Shoney's every Sunday afternoon. But we weren't. It was a pretty incredible word and there was plenty to say about it for six weeks.) One word that can mend the broken areas of our hearts so that joy might abide in the midst of our pain and comfort in our disappointment. One word that contains the peace that passes all understanding. One word: *Grace*.

At first I wondered why (or even how) he could spend so much time on one word. Later I realized that this one word—grace, and *accepting* God's grace—is where healing starts. And this healing leads to wholeness, which leads to ... well, ultimately laughter.

Years ago a good friend of mine, Dr. Nina Gunter, told a story about a little girl who brought her broken doll to a healing service at the church one night. When the invitation to come forward for healing was given, she hurried to the front with her arms full, squeezing what she carried tightly so as not to drop anything. Once she reached the altar, she laid down a tiny plastic arm that looked as if the fingers had been chewed off. Beside that she laid a tiny leg, and beside that another leg. And then she laid down the rest of the baby doll; its hair was matted, its eyes were red with rust. She knelt over the cherished toy and began to pray. The pastor went to her side and laid a reassuring arm across the little girl's shoulders. "Honey," he said, "I don't want you to be disappointed, but I'm not certain that Jesus will heal your baby doll this evening."

The young girl raised her head, seemingly surprised by the pastor's comment. "Oh, I know he won't heal my baby doll," she said, "but I do know he will heal my broken heart."

Now *that's* accepting God's grace.

Not long after that I saw a marquee in front of a church that read, "God can heal a broken heart if he's given all the pieces."

Now *that's* accepting God's grace.

And it's not easy gathering up all these broken pieces of your heart—pieces gathered as a result of a marriage filled with pain and unforgiveness, or as a result of a friend who hurt you, or because of a job you didn't get (or a job you did get and now hate), or (like Elizabeth) because of the death of loved ones (her children)—and give them all to God.

But Anne Morrow Lindbergh wrote in her book *The Steep Ascent*, "Lost (wasted) time was like a run in a stocking. It always got worse."

So don't waste another minute. You can spend your time doing nothing or you can reach out and *receive*—grasp hold of—God's grace. Can you begin to *trust God* with one small piece of your broken heart? Let him see one ugly scar. Let him heal one scratch. Lay the pieces out there like baby doll parts and allow him to do his work of grace. Grace is an incredible gift from a loving Father who has fashioned our days and loves us just the way we are. Grace says, Relax. Let go and let God work.

Perhaps it's time to fill your time with God's grace. And if you do, you know what that can eventually lead to: laughter—the kind of laughter I heard from Elizabeth that day.

Seven

Bless What Home?

I am the door of the sheep.
John 10:7 (KJV)

Not long ago, in the summer of 1997, I flew to Grand Forks, North Dakota. Only a few months before, an ark would have been the best way to get there. You see, this small community, only a few months before, had experienced what many in the media termed the "flood of the century."

That winter Grand Forks and East Grand Forks, Minnesota, had struggled through eight separate blizzards that left a snow accumulation of almost 100 inches. Then they braced themselves for the spring thaw. All that water had to go somewhere. So they prepared for the worst, building sandbag walls, higher and higher—walls that would eventually prove useless. They hadn't imagined how bad "the worst" could be.

The river came, smoothing over the city's seams—streets and bridges and parks and cemeteries—creating an even, level canvass of ruddy brown, spotted only by tent-shaped rooftops. The residents, with tired and achy muscles, could only watch helplessly as the levees gave in. Most moved to higher ground and waited. Others floated about for the duration, rescuing people and animals who had moved to the second level of their homes.

For months after the water receded, everyone—all ages, all sizes—tried to clean away the mud that marked and ruined all it came in contact with: clothes, shoes, pictures, furniture, appliances, and toys. Of nearly 2,500 homes in Grand Forks alone, only eight escaped flood damage. Lives had been lost. Livestock had been destroyed. As a result of broken gas lines, city buildings had burned and their ashes washed down the river.

This is where I was going as part of a crusade team. Dr. Ralph Bell would be preaching at one of the many "satellite" crusades conducted by the Billy Graham Evangelistic Association. I had worked with Dr. Bell and his team many times before. But now? In the aftermath of this crisis? I wasn't flying in to deliver a pressure-washer, rubber boots, or shovels. (These are what the people really needed.) I had no food rations or first-aid supplies. I had no truck to haul away the debris or to help build. I was going to Grand Forks to make people laugh. Dr. Bell's confidence in me—to invite me here—was overwhelming. The prospect of rebuilding the city seemed easier than my task. What was I going to say?

I stared at the clouds out the plane window and mentally ran through some of the news clips I'd seen in the past weeks, trying to prepare myself for meeting the people. I remembered tired, haggard, muddy faces. I remembered aerial shots of gray rooftops, all creased down the middle like greeting cards arranged on a brown table—except for the churches. Spirals and steeples and crosses and peaks all jutted up from the brown water. Seeing such evidence of the church below the water, my heart had gone out to the pastors and their families. Now I thought, *Some of them will be at the crusade tonight. Maybe they'll tell me real stories of what happened after the water went down.*

Once the plane landed, I was unexpectedly struck with—the smell. It was now August. The water had receded months ago, but the smell lingered as a pungent reminder that something terrible had happened here. Pastor Paul Knight said it was result of the aromatic concoction of mud and sludge and dead livestock and raw sewage. (I've always wondered what that would smell like.)

As we drove to the hotel, I perused the landscape. Places that should have been teeming with people, like a laundromat and a grocery store, were empty. "Where are the people?" I wondered. "Maybe no one will show up tonight." Furniture and appliances that should have been inside were now on people's front porches. Windows were broken. Debris was piled in yards, and all the buildings had a river-colored tinge. Someone had spray painted *X*s across the doors of abandoned buildings and row after row of houses. (The *X* meant demolition, the driver explained.) One bitter message painted on the side of a condemned house struck me to the core: "God Bless What Home?"

We Shoot Comedians

I checked into my room and called home to let David know I had arrived safely. I was suddenly even more terrified of the job at hand.

"Is everyone doing okay?" I asked.

"Yeah, sure. The cops ate up all our junk food, so I'll probably have to go to the store later." (He's always joking like that!)

"Did Zach get his homework finished?"

"Just before he turned on the television."

"And Chera? Did she clean her room?"

"Honey, you know that's an ongoing project. How's North Dakota?"

What could I say over the phone that could relay what I had already seen? He knew that there had been a flood, and he knew that it was over—or at least the water was gone. I decided to save all the descriptions for later. I simply said, "This is not a very funny place."

"It is now because you're there." (Thanks for reminding me.) "Just do what you do. I'm sure that's why they asked you to come along. I would stay away from the Noah jokes though. People might be a little sensitive."

"David?" (I had learned to selectively ignore some things he says.)

"Yes?"

I paused and then let the silence grow as I sorted through these new thoughts. That was home: David, Chera and Zachary, not plaster and brick. That's what I reminded myself. I didn't know if the people of Grand Forks had thought that yet, but that's what I had learned already in my short time there.

"Just pray for me," I said. "I'm going down to the coffee shop to get some lunch."

The lone waitress who helped me was very pleasant and good at what she did. (She kept filling my cup without my even asking.) During one fill-up I asked her, "So did your house survive the flood?" (I thought it was a little better than "Where were you when the lights went out?")

She told me that she and her husband had been fortunate to live in a high-rise apartment building on the campus of the University of North Dakota during the flood. But she had relatives and friends who had lost virtually everything; they'd simply packed up their few surviving boxes and left town. We talked for a bit, and I invited her to the crusade. Then she asked what I was afraid someone would ask me. I knew it was coming, and I was not looking forward to telling her—the answer alone had some ring of insensitivity to it. "So, what do you do for a living?"

I lowered my head and spoke softly into my coffee cup. "I'm a comedian."

"You're a what!?"

Even softer: "A comedian."

"Wow, I guess we could use a few laughs around here. Good luck." She might as well have said, "Wow, we shoot comedians around here—run for cover."

Sneakers in Heaven

Early that evening I stood in the backstage area of the beautiful Fine Arts auditorium, just at the edge of the staging so that I could see the people as they came in. I sighed several times, thinking about what these people had been through and how was I going to fit into this story. The security guard must have heard my sighs. He asked, "You ever get nervous?"

"Sure, I do," I told him. (My mother taught me to always tell the truth, especially to kind police officers!) "How 'bout you? You get nervous on your job?"

"Sure," he said. That seemed to exhaust our capacity for small talk.

So I jumped right into the deep stuff. "How're things with you since the flood?"

"We're holding up okay. We lost a lot. Hit pretty hard. The tough thing is, I come to work and I clean up the mess. Then I go home and do the same, every evening. There's just no end in sight. It's tough on my wife right now. She has to wash the clothes, the dishes, and everything else in the upstairs bathtub."

I really wanted to cheer him up, so I said, "Well, tell your wife that could be handy. She can get all of her housework done while she soaks in the tub."

He grinned. (Not the laugh I had wanted. Not the chuckle I had hoped for—just a grin. Now I *was* nervous.)

Before I knew it, I was sitting on the platform—with the other members of our team and also with local leaders: a Minnesota senator, the mayor of East Grand Forks, and the mayor of Grand Forks, whom I recognized from television.

We sang choruses, praise and worship, and I watched the people sing—some with faces turned to heaven, some with hands raised to heaven, but just about all wearing brand-new white sneakers. It seems an athletic shoe company had donated thousands of shoes to this community. I was watching their feet, thinking, *If we wear sneakers in heaven, then this is what it'll look like*, when someone called my name, so I slipped out of my chair and took the microphone.

I'm not sure where some of my words come from, and that happens to me a lot. It makes my husband so terribly nervous! We talk about the plan for the evening, the topics, the list of jokes, the songs I'm going to sing, and then nine times out of ten I do something different. Something just comes over me! (I think it's the same "something" that used to terrify my mother when I was a kid and someone would hand me a microphone.) I looked at the crowd, gave them a big Tennessee hello and said, "Ya'll make me feel right at home up here 'cause down in Tennessee we got lots of appliances in our front yards too."

And they laughed. Not a grin, not a chuckle. But a good old laugh out loud. And it sounded wonderful.

After a few minutes of fun, I stepped to the far edge of the platform, as close as I could get to them, and told them how honored and how inspired I was to see their faces. I confessed that there was no way I could ever know what it was like to walk the same, muddy road as they had, but I shared with them a story or two from my life's journey. I spoke of Charlotta's death and Cheralyn's. I mentioned Dad's leaving and of more recent struggles. And then I sang one of my favorite old hymns, "He Hideth My Soul."

Immediately following my portion, Dr. Ralph Bell delivered one of the most powerful messages I have ever heard. In his booming, clear voice he introduced the title of his message. It was a question: "Does God love Grand Forks, North Dakota?" I almost stopped breathing. I couldn't believe he had just said that. How many times, I wondered, had people in this city whispered that thought? Does God love us? Where is God when it hurts? Where is God in the midst of this disaster?

As the words rolled across Dr. Bell's lips, the Holy Spirit mingled among the broken and tired citizens in that room and brought the greatest refrain of peace and real hope into the hearts of the people there. As the praise and worship group sang "Come, Just As You Are" and the invitation was given, people poured toward the front, accepting the hope offered in Jesus. From the corner of my eye, I noticed some people leave the platform and go to the front for prayer. I recognized those faces—the city mayors.

Hope Still Floats

It is hard to have the right words for someone who desperately feels as if God's clock has stopped ticking at the worst possible time. In Grand Forks I met Pastor Dan Klug, who has had a whole series of losses. He lost his mother a few years ago. And then his police-officer brother was killed in May 1996. Then the winter blizzards, then the floods, which devastated his congregation and his own home.

After being with the people of this community, seeing them, speaking to them, and listening to them, I wasn't so much concerned about what had happened during the flood as I was with what was going to happen now—after the flood. Pastor Klug was spic-and-span clean, even had on some new sneakers, but I could see the river had colored his countenance. I asked him, "How do you dish out any hope on Sunday morning?"

He took a deep breath, something I imagined him doing thousands of times over the last few months, and answered, "I guess you just have to be real. Be honest. There have been Sundays when I just get up and preach what I know, convincing myself, I know this. I don't feel this—but I know this."

Isn't that what faith is all about? Remember what the writer of Hebrews said, as he introduced a long list of spiritual giants who themselves walked through the valley of the shadow of hardship and death. "Now faith is being sure of what we hope for and certain of what we do not see. This is what the ancients were commended for" (Hebrews 11:1–2).

The mother of Moses is someone I look forward to meeting in heaven. I'll bet she's a lot like my mom: short, plump, cries when you talk about the Lord. And what faith it must have taken for her to hide her new baby in the bulrushes: "By faith Moses' parents hid him for three months after he was born" (Hebrews 11:23). She could have been bitter—especially believing the king was going to kill her child, especially after having to give away her child just to save his life, especially after watching her son being raised as the son of someone else. (I think she could use a good hug around the neck, and I—or Mom—will give her one.) But the mother of Moses did not grow bitter. She continued to praise God.

I can read the story about Moses and how his mother shipped him off in a basket and pretend to understand how she simply gave it all to God and went about her daily business over the years until Moses was grown and he returned gray-headed and singing "Let My People Go." But every year for her was filled with 365 days— sometimes more—and each day was filled with the memory of pain, loneliness, devastation, and loss. Each day was another opportunity to be bitter—or better. Choose you this day to be bitter or better. Can I give you a hint? I've learned that better may take a lot more work (you may have to build a crib that floats, fend off the croco-diles, push through the bulrushes), but the end result is much more liberating than sarcastic bitterness.

Better, Not Bitter

A few months later I returned to Grand Forks for a special retreat. There was less mud, and the sneakers had been broken in. I also got to experience Pastor Dan Klug's sense of humor. He and Pastor Knight sat on the front row during my performance, exer-cising their special "gifts." (They made silly kindergarten faces at me the whole time!)

When I had the chance, I asked Pastor Dan, "How in the world do you cope?" I wanted to know what has made him better not bitter.

He grinned. "I just tell myself, 'Hang on, Dan. This is where God is going to do his work.' In my own heart. In the hearts of his people."

Pastor Dan said he looked forward to the day when people from his congregation could "load up and go to minister to people in another city who may be going through some type of similar dev-astation. Now that will be an exciting sign of healing."

I thought—but now wish I'd said—"Believe me, you guys have ministered to me and an entire nation—as your story of faith-fulness spreads—and you didn't have to go anywhere."

The writer of Hebrews teaches us one more thing about the faithful giants: "These were all commended for their faith, yet none of them received what had been promised. God had planned some-thing better for us so that only together with us would they be made perfect" (11:39–40).

God had planned something better? Yes. You see, in God's per-fect timing, he sent Jesus the Son from his heavenly home to earth—to the womb of a woman. (Maybe it's like Moses' parents putting him in a dark, covered basket to float out into the bul-rushes.) To a world that was marked condemned.

"God bless what home?" By coming to earth as one of us—suffering with us, even unto death—God did bless this home. This city. This world.

The redemption—the ultimate blessing—is not complete, but the critical victory was won—when Jesus rose from the grave, when he stood at the door of his own tomb and said to Mary Magdalene: "Woman, why are you crying?"

If you, like me when I was young and angry, are still in a place where you're saying "God bless what home?"—I ask you to consider another piece of graffiti that I saw in that devastated city of Grand Forks.

I was on my way to the airport. I was going home, leaving behind this devastation that for many was (and is) home. Here and there I would see someone, usually wearing gloves, tossing something bulky, and usually brown, into the back of a truck. Many of the houses I had seen before, marked with an *X*, were gone now. Only empty lots and some scattered debris remained.

On one such lot, barren of even shade trees, was evidence of a house. All that remained was a crumbling block foundation and a single doorframe and door, where a family had probably greeted guests. With black spray paint, someone had written in big bold letters—for all the world to see: Jesus is the door.

Eight

Every Woman Needs a Dry-Clean-Only Dress

There is now no condemnation for those who are in Christ Jesus.
Romans 8:1

Have you ever really embarrassed yourself?" she asked me. Her name is December. Her family calls her Dee. At the time she was a twenty-year-old, very pregnant preacher's kid. I met her while speaking to a small ladies group in California. "Sure I have! Which time would you like to hear about?"

One time in particular came to mind rather quickly. So I leaned forward in my seat and shared with the group, anxious to hear them laugh.

It was a special night on the Grand Ole Opry. They were highlighting several country comedians and had invited me to share a few funny lines with the likes of Jerry Clower, Grandpa Jones, and Mike Snider. This news in itself would have been enough to cause me to lose a few nights' sleep—and about six pounds (I always lose weight when I get nervous).

But then the secretary at the Opry called to tell me not to be in a hurry to leave when the show was over. She said (and I quote), "Stick around after your segment, because Johnny Russell wants you guys to go out together at the end."

Out? With me!? I thought. Wow! This is more than gracious of the folks at the Opry. Johnny Russell is one of the greatest entertainers and songwriters on the Opry. This is the man who wrote "Walkin' on New Grass" and "Fourteen Karat Mind." I couldn't believe we were all going to go out together! "Wonder where we're going?" I said to David. And who-all would be in the group? Maybe we'd go to some secret hideaway known only to the great legends of country music. Maybe we'd take a fancy ride in a limo to one of Nashville's hot spots and people would take pictures and we'd be on the cover of a magazine, laughing with food in our mouths. Oh, the possibilities! "This calls for a new dress. Perhaps even a Dry-Clean-Only dress!"

Don't you hate learning really important things when a lot of other people are around to watch? That night I learned that what we sometimes hear is not what is actually said—much like the man who told his wife, "Wow, honey, there is a lot of print on that particular fabric." But what did she hear? "Whoa! That material makes you look like a giant flower garden!"

Or like Uncle Lemmie—who doesn't hear too well. One day he was listening to a sermon on the second coming of Christ. In the middle of the sermon the preacher, one of those with a down-home style, spoke directly to the congregation: "Your time is limited!"

Uncle Lemmie jumped up and said, "You've got fifteen more minutes!"

Whoa! You should have seen them scramble to the altar.

Uncle Lemmie couldn't figure what the fuss was about. He was just giving the preacher what he asked for. He thought the preacher had said, "What time is it, Lemmie?"

Back to my own story—that night at the Opry, as I walked down the backstage hallway (with my new dress lying in a wrinkle-free position in the trunk of my car), I spotted the secretary—the one I had talked with earlier—checking some notes of last-minute details for the live show. I couldn't stand the suspense any longer. I slipped up to her and introduced myself. We chatted for a moment about comedy on the Opry, and then I asked her, "June, how do you think I should dress for dinner? And do you know where we might be going when we 'go out together'?"

She looked a little confused. (That's when I first thought I might be in trouble—I was already regretting having taken the tags off the dress.) She said, "Oh, honey, not out to eat together! OUT—on stage—to take a bow together at the end of the show!"

Sometimes moments of miscommunication can be funny. Sometimes it is simply an opportunity to get a new dress. And then there are times when communication breaks down and hurt and pain go to work, building their walls, hardening hearts and causing those who are hurt to ask more than once, "Why?"

December's Story

Some of the ladies laughed at my story. December tried. I wondered what was going on with her. I knew she was a preacher's kid. And I recognized the weight on her shoulders—although I had no idea what caused it.

But a little later in the weekend, December told me her story, colored with pain and disappointment and disillusionment. She is so much like the "typical" PKs I have noticed in the past five years of working with adult preacher's kids. Many deal with the unfortunate feeling of never being accepted. Many carry the burden and fear that they will somehow ruin their dads' ministries. Many grow up thinking that everyone's feelings, emotions, and spiritual well-being are much more important than their own. They are so afraid they will do something so terrible that the church people will turn on them and, more fearfully, that their parents will turn on them. December summed it up when she said to me: "Why is it that we have such compassion for the lost, but when one of 'our own' makes a mistake, there goes the compassion?"

Here's her story. "I was twelve when I decided I could never do anything to make them (the church) happy," said December. "I even overheard some of the ladies saying, 'Look at December. She is nothing but trouble.' So I stopped caring about the church because I was sure they didn't care about me."

In her early teens, December rebelled. And then she ran away. "By the time I was seventeen, I was a homeless teen who slept in my parked car on the streets of San Jose," she said. She was desperately looking for some kind of affirmation, some kind of love without conditions and rules. She frequented dance clubs. "I gave my body to men I barely knew," she admitted.

"As awful as my experience with church had been, something drew me back. While on the nightclub and sex circuit, I would slip into the back of my parents' church on Sunday mornings. My dad and I would often meet eyes as he preached, and I would slip out before the service ended. My guilt overwhelmed me. Though I could see the church had grown more loving, I thought I could never clean up enough to please the members, my parents, or God."

Eventually her looking for love in all the wrong places left her alone—and pregnant. "When I told the baby's father I was pregnant, he walked out of my life. I sinned a lot, but I couldn't bring myself to abort this baby."

And then she walked an even more precarious tightrope—needing her family, yet feeling like she had embarrassed her father; needing the church, but feeling like an outcast. "I just knew they wouldn't forgive me."

She had spent a lot of time running from what she thought would be a horrible reaction from her parents. Perhaps she had misunderstood. Perhaps she had thought that her parents cared about everyone else more than her.

Eventually, knowing her parents and church members would find out about her pregnancy, she knew she "had to face Mom and Dad."

The next Monday December met her parents in her dad's church office. Her hands trembled. She just knew that what she was about to tell them would destroy their ministry and crush their last hope for her. She lowered herself into a chair and drew a mouthful of air.

"This morning I need a parent, not a pastor," she started.

But before she could finish, her dad interrupted: "I already know you're pregnant, Dee," he said. Her jaw dropped. She was glad she was sitting. "This morning," her father continued, "God prepared me for your news."

After a short silence, December began to weep. Her parents drew near and hugged her close. "The tension in my head and stomach escaped through my tears," she explained to me. "I was completely broken."

Her mom broke the awkward silence, speaking just the right words at just the right time: "You'd better eat something, Dee. You've got to nourish our baby."

That day real healing began in that girl's heart.

Forgiving Ourselves

Dee's story reminds me of the Prodigal Son and his godly father. I wonder if the young man's departure, which led to sin, was prompted by a whole community of people thinking he would just never measure up, so he went out to prove them wrong. Could that be what he thought? You never quite know about those lines of miscommunication, misunderstanding. (What did that raised eyebrow really mean?) And then one thing led to another and little resentments and medium-sized rebellions left unchecked turned to significant sins that left him convinced that he was utterly unworthy of being let back in his father's house.

But yet he chose to turn around and go home—to walk down that road, ready to beg his father's mercy. And the father—representing our heavenly Father—welcomed the repentant heart home.

As Dee turned to God, she sensed his forgiveness. As she returned to her family, they sensed God directing them to welcome her. She told me, "The bottom line is that I came back to my family and God because they loved me with no strings attached. They forgave me. I knew they cared. I thought I could do something to make them disown me, but I was wrong."

My funny story from the Opry was about a time when my own miscommunication led to a hilarious laugh together. But what happens when assumptions don't lead to a laugh—but to bad choices and ultimately sin, where our embarrassment can lead us into a lifetime of guilt?

December's mom had already forgiven her—had accepted her. But December was slow to forgive herself. I think sometimes we struggle with forgiving ourselves because we believe there is no home to run to. December believed that; yet that weekend I witnessed her and her mother talking, listening to each other, embracing and—yes, you guessed it—even laughing together. I witnessed the sweet relief that forgiveness brings. When December's mom forgave her, December could see home. But only after December was able to forgive herself could she truly believe the mat at the front door: Welcome.

Perhaps December wasn't asking me, "Have you ever embarrassed yourself?" but maybe, "Have you ever had to learn to forgive yourself for doing something you really regret—whether it's sin (that calls for repentance) or being immature or contributing your fair share to a misunderstanding or . . . ?"

I have struggled personally with forgiving myself for what sometimes seemed like the silliest of incidents. I remember sneaking into Cheralyn's room one afternoon and finding her diary open on her bed. I couldn't resist. I sat down and began reading. Later I teased her about her secret thoughts about her boyfriend—with him in the room! Maybe if we could have grown old together, we could have looked back and laughed about the incident one day, but we never got the chance.

I carried the guilt around for weeks. Although in my heart I know that Cheralyn had died knowing how much I adored her, loved her, and how sorry I was to have teased her the week before she got sick, I still hated myself for reading her diary.

So if I struggled with the guilt of something as silly as that, can you imagine my struggles with the guilt of sin? Can I share with you a couple of verses that were written to Christians that have helped me tremendously? "If we claim to be without sin, we deceive ourselves and the truth is not in us. If we confess our sins, he is faithful and just and will forgive us our sins and purify us from all unrighteousness" (1 John 1:8–9).

Our sins need to be confessed; God asks us to turn from them and walk in holiness. We may need to apologize to someone. We may need to make amends. But sometimes we are just being too hard on ourselves. Read this next Scripture closely. It comes just a page after 1 John 1:9: "Dear children, let us not love with words or tongue but with actions and in truth. This then is how we know that we belong to the truth, and how we *set our hearts at rest* in his presence whenever our hearts condemn us. For God is greater than our hearts, and he knows everything. Dear friends, if our hearts do not condemn us, we have confidence before God and receive from him anything we ask, because we obey his commands and do what pleases him (1 John 3:18–22, emphasis mine).

Bagging the Guilt

Sometimes we may need a bit of help to get rid of "false guilt" that we carry unnecessarily. Let me take you back to Grand Forks, North Dakota. I had a long conversation with Pastor Dan Klug, who gave me his version of "the great flood."

"I had been out sandbagging, checking on parishioners, stopping all over town, and trying to help. We knew the minutes were ticking. I have never been so exhausted in my life. I got home at about 5:30 A.M., and just as I dozed off, I heard the trucks outside. They were shutting off all the gas lines. For the rest of the day I heard sirens all around town because one dike had broken—and then another. I spent the day trying to call and find out where some of my church members were, helping the elderly members.

"That evening it dawned on me that I hadn't really prepared for the flood at my house. So my wife and I spent the remainder of the day putting everything on tables and putting sandbags around the backyard. When there was nothing else to do, I stood in the backyard and watched the water coming our way.

"There's a golf course behind my house, but I couldn't see it anymore. Just water. I took a seven wedge out of my golf bag and started hitting golf balls as far as I could into the tops of trees in the middle of the murky water. Several neighbors saw what I was doing and came over, and we all took turns whacking balls into the river. We'd just stand there and watch them drop into the water.

"A friend of mine who works for the city of East Grand Forks thought I'd get maybe three or four inches on the main floor. It was 2 A.M. when the sirens went off in our neighborhood. I still can't believe the water got to us. I woke up my wife, we threw some clothes in the car, grabbed the dogs, and got in the long line of traffic heading out of town."

He told me this months after the flood. I remembered seeing on the news the church steeples reaching up above the drowning water, so I asked him, "When was the last time you went by the church—before you were evacuated?"

Silence. A tear rolled down his face. "You know, I feel so guilty about that, but when the siren went off, I just got my family out. That night I sat on the edge of the hotel bed, and put my head in my hands and sobbed. I couldn't believe I didn't go by there. I felt so terrible about that."

This pastor was carrying guilt he was never meant to bear. I reached across the table and placed my hand on his wrist and said, "Pastor Dan, from one preacher's kid who had occasions to feel like the church, the building, even the over-flowing toilets and the ladies who didn't like me, all came first, can I tell you this from the bottom of my heart? You did absolutely the right thing."

We both sat there and cried. I cried because I remembered what it was like to carry the guilt of my past. And he cried because someone had given him permission to forgive himself, which in turn "set his heart at rest."

You see, Christ died for us to bring us hope and forgiveness. Peace and joy. Release from the pain of the past—to set our hearts at rest whenever our hearts condemn us. Did you hear that verse in 1 John? Do not misconstrue these words—no miscommunication here: "God is greater than our heart, and he knows everything." And when we embrace his love and in turn extend it to others, we amazingly find ourselves living a happier life.

Corrie ten Boom described what God does with our mistakes. "He is the greatest artist, but we must surrender. Surrender your blunders to the Lord. He can use them to make the pattern of your life more beautiful."

Before we turn the page, let me give you a PS to December's story. Several months after our visit, I received a beautiful letter from her, along with a picture of a gorgeous baby boy. Today her church family is rallying around this parsonage family, supporting them, loving them, and laughing with them.

Joy has come into their hearts because they have witnessed God's mercy and grace in action. New life came into the world in the form of a little boy and into Dee's new life in the form of Christ, who brings forgiveness and peace after the storm—sunshine after rain. And a hearty laugh, even when we've embarrassed ourselves!

Nine

Pepsi Cola Lake

Forget the former things; do not dwell on the past.
See, I am doing a new thing!
Isaiah 43:18–19

It happened again just last week. Someone called across the hotel lobby where I was staying and speaking for a women's function, "Hey, Chonda! I have a question for you."

I stopped and listened, prepared to respond. Sometimes people want to know what part of South Carolina I grew up in. Sometimes they want to know if we really did paint that cat to look like a skunk. And sometimes they ask me, "Whatever happened to your father?" I used to just sigh and say, "He's fine. I don't hear from him much. But he's doing fine."

I find it very difficult to talk about him, I guess because the daughter in me simply doesn't want to cause him any pain or discomfort. As far as positives go, I have made a conscious choice to hang on to memories that are sweet and pleasant, joyful and enduring. But I have decided that "feeling uncomfortable" is no longer an excuse for not talking about something. That choice, as painful as it may be sometimes, has helped healing to take place in my life— and perhaps in the lives of a few people listening.

This is a painful chapter for me to write. But I believe it may also be the most important. So many times I meet hurting people who are searching for something they can use to effect healing. Perhaps what I have learned is that "something" you can use. So as I take a deep breath and sigh, I'll not tell you that everything between my father and me is "just fine." Instead, I would like to tell you what I have come to learn about my father.

You see, my father has battled with depression for years, and from what I have witnessed, he has never acknowledged any responsibility for the pain he brought to me and my family. As a kid, especially as a teenager, I got up every day wondering, dreading, what the day might hold with my father. What will he say today? What will he do today? Is he in a good mood or a bad mood? Yet for his sake, the story that I tell you now about my father is not about what he did or said, but rather about how *I* reacted.

The Perfect Daughter

I was seventeen when my parents divorced. It was difficult to straddle that fence between a hurting mother and an angry father: I wanted my father to be happy and my mother's heart to be whole. Looking back, I see that I had walked along the top of the fence for a very long time.

When my dad first left, several weeks went by before we heard from him. Then from time to time he would just pop in, unannounced, to visit with Cheralyn and me. After Cheralyn died he came less and less. But when he did come, I discovered that something would happen to me each time: my heart rate would increase; afraid of what he might say or do, I would work myself into a frenzy to be sure that our visit was perfect—clean the house, prepare a wonderful supper with his favorite foods, make sure he was comfortable—anything to make him smile, to hear him say something nice, or to just make him want to visit again.

Shortly after their divorce was final, he remarried. As the years went by, I tried to make friends with his new wife and went to visit them on occasion. Even after I was married, I worked desperately to be a perfect daughter when he would stop by. I thought there must be something I could do to bring about the change in his heart that I longed to see. I wanted to hear him say, "I'm sorry for leaving you"; "I'm sorry for the pain I've caused you." I wanted the man on *Father Knows Best* to ring my doorbell—whole, stable, and happy. So I jumped through all the hoops, determined to fix what was broken—single-handedly. But all I accomplished was exhaustion.

I began to read books and to ask questions, trying to find out all that I could about manic depression. Somewhere along the way, some bright, intelligent, savvy counselor (my friend Alison, I believe) explained to me about the perils of manic depression (the diagnosis my father had been given years before). This information helped me to understand my father better, but none of my newfound knowledge changed him or fixed what was broken in our relationship. And what I finally had to accept is that nothing *I* ever did would.

Jesus had comforted me during my most painful days. But anger, fear, and pain still tore away at me deep inside my heart, and those emotions seemed to get worse every time my father called or popped into my life. I was so busy frantically trying to change him that I forgot to peer into my own heart at what needed to change.

God himself mercifully held me up as I tried to balance myself and walk along the top of some emotional fence, not allowing me to fall to either side and hurt myself. But eventually I needed to come down and walk on steady firm ground. Galatians 5:25 tells us, "Since we live by the Spirit, let us keep in step with the Spirit." I knew that he wanted me to come down from the fence and walk beside him in truth. In freedom. I just didn't know when or how he would prompt me to do so. But God knew.

Letting Go

It was several years after I was married. I was speaking in South Carolina (my old stomping grounds!) for Senior Adult Day during camp meeting at the Nazarene Campground in Batesburg, South Carolina. As my "routine" always seemed to go, I impersonated Minnie Pearl for about twenty minutes, slipped off my hat, and then shared some funny childhood stories from the "second row, piano side"—where my family always sat in church—and then a word of testimony to the afternoon crowd.

Later, as I took a private tour across the campgrounds, I could barely breathe. Everywhere I looked the memories of growing up surrounded me: the old log cabin I stayed in my very first week of junior camp (I was nine); the long white cafeteria building where I had eaten so many cold banana Popsicles on hot summer days at youth camp; the waterfalls where I had my first kiss; and the lake— so dark and murky that it looked like Pepsi Cola. I guess that's why we always called it Pepsi Cola Lake!

Sometimes I believed that lake and I had a lot in common. My sweet, funny stories from the second row, piano side may have been attractive and calm on the surface, and people would gather to look and smile and appreciate what God had done with part of his cre- ation, never suspecting that just beneath the surface were secrets and pain, much like the mud and scum that lay not too far down from the lake's surface.

Not far from the lake was the tabernacle where the evening ser- vices were held. Dr. Jim Deihl preached that night. In his message he used the same phrase time and again, "Choose you this day whom you will serve." I sat and listened to every word. He told about a par- ticular legal battle that illustrated a situation when circumstances just weren't right, weren't fair, and pointed out that "even as Christians, from time to time, we are caught up in a battle we never intended." He said that in some lives the issue of who's wrong and who's right may not always be clear. But there is peace through *forgiveness*. There is freedom in *forgiveness*. Even when the answers to your questions are not always clear, that's when you must, "Choose you this day whom you will serve." And you who have been forgiven greatly—you must choose to extend forgiveness. Wow!

That night the Holy Spirit nudged at my heart, and I went to the altar for prayer. I was determined to come down from the fence for good and get my footing on steady ground. And the only way to do that was to forgive my dad *first*. (Whew! This was not going to be easy!)

For years, along with the pain and fear, I had harbored an incredible amount of resentment. I had allowed the fear and anger to control me, and I knew I had to make a choice to let go of my father. I had to admit "that I cannot fix him; I cannot please him; I cannot heal his mind or bandage his heart. I cannot change the past, but I can forgive what happened in the past and move on." I had some sweet memories of my father—those I could still cherish. The others I chose to throw into the sea of forgetfulness.

I made the choice that night to let go—to forgive—but it hasn't always been easy (which I later learned is pretty normal). Valerie Bell writes in *She Can Laugh at the Days to Come*:

"I am finding that forgiving is a process. I might do well at not dwelling on my wounds for a while; I may even begin to feel some mercy toward those who have wounded me. But then it starts all over again. I remember the pain, and before I know it, I'm picking my scabs, reviewing the wrongs I have against the person who wounded me. I am no longer wishing the person well, but feeling as though they should fall into one! Sometimes the work of forgiveness seems to be a forever job. I must begin the forgiveness process all over again."

You see, for years and years, I believed I could be clever enough to fix whatever was broken or be funny enough to avoid the pain. I know now that I can't cover up or fix everything that goes wrong— not even with a good laugh—but I can let go of a piece of pain.

Forgiveness Is a Process

I turned to other people familiar with the process to help me: my pastor, my mother, and my sweet friend and counselor, Alison. During this same visit to South Carolina, I stopped by her office. (I swapped a few videos for a few moments of her time.) One moment, as I would talk, I would become so angry because I was allowing my father to control me. The next moment I was trembling and terri- fied at how I was reacting. Then suddenly, without warning, I would weep and grieve for a father to hold me and then weep and grieve because I believed I may have hurt the one I had. (I had become a real acrobat on top of that fence!)

Alison made me write letters that week. I wrote some painful ones, some angry ones, some sassy ones, and many letters filled with tears. I needed to speak the truth, how I really felt and how I needed to . . . forgive. There it was again! That was my ladder off this fence: forgiveness. Why hadn't I heard about this earlier—like years ear- lier? Alison just smiled.

At first I was afraid, hesitant to forgive because I thought that meant I would be required to reenter a relationship that I sensed was not good for me, a relationship that I could not repair. But I learned that forgiveness means letting go, not necessarily going back. Letting go. I could do that.

When Alison was satisfied that I had exhausted all my feelings into these letters, we burned them all in a little metal bucket she kept in her office for just such occasions. On my way home from South Carolina that week, I stopped once more at the edge of the old murky waters of Pepsi Cola Lake and tossed a bucket full of ashes into my sea of forgetfulness. Although throwing away those ashes was a sweet event commemorating my desire to be better not bitter (actually, the whole event wasn't as dramatic as I would have liked: some of the burnt pages flew back into the grass, some into my face, but most of them did make it to the water, where they spun about and eventually sank), forgiveness is still a process, not an event.

As the days go by, I can now laugh with Valerie Bell as she writes, "I am not a woman who is conformed to my pain, whose self-definition is the litany of sins that has been committed against me, who would have little left were I to lose it. No. I am a woman whose soul is forming to God. I cannot control how others treat me, but I can control my own response. I choose to relate to others based on my own character, not theirs. That is a tremendously freeing concept! My soul, formed in its 'becoming' to the dimensions of God's love, can extend forgiveness even when the other person is not worthy, never says the word 'sorry,' or ever shows a grain of remorse."

Occasionally when fear causes those ashes to drift my way, or sorrow pushes them near my shore, I remind myself of the day and the hour (it's written in the back of my Bible) that I chose to climb down from the fence—to forgive my father—to throw our struggles into Pepsi Cola Lake and walk on.

Choosing to Be Better

In recent years I have learned even more about forgiveness as I host an annual Conference for Adult Preachers' Kids. For the

most part the weekend is a celebration of our heritage. We are kin-
dred spirits who have come to a place where we can laugh about the
sights and sounds and stories we share. But once in awhile we meet
some PKs who can find very little even to smile about. They're
stuck, confused about who God is, disappointed by Christian people
who somewhere along their way treated them a little less human—
simply because they were born into the pastor's family.

Each year we invite Tim Sanford and David Gatewood to our
conference. They are both PKs—preachers' kids. Added to that
they're MKs—missionaries' kids. They're both psychologists who
have their own private practices and also work for Focus on the
Family. Every session they present is coated in the reality that healing and forgiveness go hand in hand. In Tim's book *I Have to Be
Perfect! (And Other Parsonage Heresies)*, he writes what forgiveness is
not and what it is:

"Forgiveness is not an event where you utter pious words that
somehow release the accused, and yourself as well. It is not denying
the wrong ever occurred. It is not forgetting the events of your past
ever took place. It is not a spiritual way of saying that the wrong to
you is all right and of no consequence.

"It is not self-martyrdom. It is not cheap, quick or easy. It is
not automatically trusting or even liking the person who hurt you.
These are all things that forgiveness is not.

"Now let's talk about what it is.

"In the Hebrew, which is a picture language, the word forgiveness looks like this: To burn. To carry away. To bear or endure.
To pardon from penalty. To suffer. (Ouch!) To lift off the weight of
burden. In Greek: To forsake. To lay aside. To put away. To yield
up. To sustain damage. To send away from me.

"Forgiveness is to lift off the weight of the debt, to send it away
and to absorb or suffer the damage myself. Forgiveness is a process,
not an event. It takes time for a 'process' to process. Healing and
forgiveness both take time."

I think there are other times when we can grow so accustomed
to our misery that we'd rather just hang on to the anger and pain.

We've learned to eat, sleep, and live on top of a narrow fence—and, after all, we've handled it thus far. Besides, it is all that we know, and the unknown may be a bit scarier than the familiar.

Allow me to mix my metaphors: Those who choose to stay behind their protective walls of anger—walls sometimes disguised with sarcastic laughter—those are the ones who lose the most. I love this quote from Evelyn Bence's book *Leaving Home*:

"Who would I be if I were no longer angry, for my anger, in a sense defined me? Without it I might . . . lose my creativity. I might lose my intensity, which I saw as some kind of wall that kept me separated from the rest of the world. I would have to deal with the hole that would be left when the anger vacated. And the size of the hole frightened me."

If I could, I would hug Evelyn's neck and laugh with sweet joy and say, "The hole has been filled with 'joy unspeakable'—full of glory!" Because today I choose to forgive and walk on. Today I choose to be better. Today and forevermore, I choose Jesus. Today.

But not every package is finished off with a perfectly tied bow; not every story ends "happily ever after." The freedom that the "forgiveness process" brings allows us to create not a fence, but a boundary. On one side lies the pain and anger that we choose no longer to visit. And on the other side, we "walk in step with the spirit." And me? I put on my hiking boots a long time ago.

So the next time someone asks me about my father, believe me when I say, "He's just fine. Really, he *is* just fine."

Ten

Take Two Laughs and Call Me in the Morning

A happy heart makes the face cheerful, but heartache crushes the spirit.
Proverbs 15:13

When my mother married again—to a wonderful man named Sammy Farless—we all rejoiced. The only people crying at their reception were her grandchildren (and that was because their diapers needed changing—it had been a long day at Ponderosa steak house!). My stepfather, Papaw Sam, is so funny. He doesn't mean to be. But he is!

When Papaw was about forty, his brother took him to a health spa—for the first time ever. Their plan was to get in shape, to feel better, to live longer, to look good. They decided to warm up their muscles a bit by jogging around the indoor track—a wide lane neatly carpeted with arrows pointing each runner in the right direction.

When Papaw tells the story, he'll wave his arms and say, "The whole room was walled with mirrors." This made the small gym seem giant. "I started running and got about halfway around and noticed this fella coming right at me. I sped up, but he kept coming and then—" BLAM! Papaw ran right into the mirror!

A mild concussion and a few stitches later, Papaw Sam kept saying, "I thought that guy was going to get out of the way."

My family loves to tell and retell that story around the Christmas tree. I can just hear the laughter. Zach has a tiny cackle much like me. Chera will usually talk during her laughs: "Oh me . . .

You've got to be kidding." David is just a grinner. Mom gets so tickled I'm afraid sometimes she will pass out. And Papaw Sam will hee-
hee-hee (even at the part where he runs into himself).

The Universal Language

So let's talk a bit about laughter—in its many guises. If you
think about it, it's a universal language that needs no interpreter. I
have watched this incredible gift called laughter for many years. Not
everyone can play the piano. Not everyone can sing or paint or
sculpt images from clay. These forms of special gifts have been
doled out sparingly. But laughter! It comes in all shapes and sizes!
It is a gift God has given to all of us. No special tools are required.
Not even a practice run is necessary. As Boyce Rensberger notes,
"Language is learned but not laughter. In infancy, the ability to
laugh appears . . . long before speech" ("But Seriously, Folks. . .What
Is Laughter?" *Washington Post*, September 10, 1997).

And have you ever really thought about what laughter *looks*
like? Rensberger tries to imagine how laughter might be perceived
by a martian anthropologist studying alien earthlings. First these
already odd-looking creatures (humans) break from their dull,
monotonous tones (talking) into some sort of spasms that shake and
quake their shoulders and sometimes even their whole bodies. They
bare their teeth and wrinkle their noses. . . .

And I can imagine, if the Martians watched long enough, they
would report back that some of these earthlings would be quick to
cover their mouths with one hand or both hands. Others would
throw their heads back and leave their mouths wide open and clear.
They'd slap their knees, point, wave, or put both hands on their
waists to keep their bellies still. The aliens would probably agree
that these humans engage in a very odd, varied, and extremely physical activity.

That's what laughter might look like to one who has never
seen it. Then there's what you hear. The sounds of laughter can be
as varied as the songs of birds in a forest. As I said in the prologue,
I collect laughs like others collect marbles or butterflies. My father-

in-law had a laugh that sounded like a wind-up toy winding down: lots of fast, strong hee-hee-hees at first that would slowly fade to nothing until he could catch his breath and start again.

And I remember this big, wide man who worked at a department store I used to go to who was a perfect example of a "blaster." No matter how funny the moment or the joke, the most laugh I ever heard from him would be no more than a single, loud (booming, actually) "Ha!" That was it. One blast so strong it expended all the emotion and energy of the hilarious moment.

And then there is the "killer laugher." I say killer because if you are sitting too close to this type of laugher, you can get hurt—or worse. My sister-in-law Doris is like that. When she laughs, she swats at whatever or whomever is near. It's not safe to be funny around her.

When I get to heaven I want to hear the laughter of some of those biblical characters. And I mean characters. What did David sound like when he danced for joy before the ark of the Lord? And I'll bet Noah laughed after he docked the ark and watched the last of the animals trot off into the forest. Shadrach, Meshach, and Abednego must have had a good laugh together once things cooled down. And surely Adam laughed when he first saw the orangutans.

And then there's Sarah. After waiting "forever" for a baby, she laughed sarcastically when she was told she'd have one. But when that baby was born, Sarah laughed again. Only this time it was a good hearty laugh—from the right place. I imagine it was a pure, heartwarming guffaw. Genesis 21:6–7 gives her short laughter speech—at the baby's circumcision: "God has brought me laughter, and everyone who hears about this will laugh with me." And she added, "Who would have said to Abraham that Sarah would nurse children? Yet I have borne him a son in his old age."

And she laughed. And she collected that laugh to be used again and again. She knew that every time she called her child's name to come in and wash his hands for supper, she would be reminded to laugh—because she had named that little bundle of joy Isaac, which means "laughter."

The Best Medicine

Laughter is as cleansing to me as a good cry and less expensive—if you consider the cost of mascara. Remember the words of Proverbs 17:22? "A cheerful heart is good medicine, but a crushed spirit dries up the bones." I like the good old King James Version: "A merry heart doeth good like a medicine." Solomon knew it four thousand years ago. A man named Robert Burton realized it four hundred years ago. In a book titled *Anatomy of Melancholy*, he notes "humor purges the blood, making the body young, lively, and fit for any manner of employment."

Author Norman Cousins visited Albert Schweitzer at his hospital in Africa. In his now classic *Anatomy of an Illness*, Cousins says, "Schweitzer employed humor as a form of equatorial therapy, a way of reducing the temperatures and the humidity and the tensions." When his staff gathered for dinner, Schweitzer served up a funny story. "Laughter at the dinner hour was probably the most important course," he says. Cousins concludes, "Humor at Lambarene was vital nourishment."

Actually, it's only been very recently that scientific studies confirm that laughter can be helpful to your health. At the Primary Health Care Center in Motala, Sweden, Dr. Lars Ljungdahl (with a name like that, you need a good sense of humor) conducts laugh therapy. Over years of research he has determined that laughter suppresses the hormones that cause stress. Laughter actually reduces pain. (So next time you stub your toe, try laughing.) And a good laugh (a snort, a blast, a hee-hee-hee, whatever) increases the blood flow to the brain and the oxygen level in the arteries and veins by releasing valuable endorphins into the body. These endorphins act like a "brain-made" drug that sets off biological processes that make people feel good—immediately.

Dr. Ljungdahl believes his research is universally applicable. He says, "The people of Motala, Sweden have a reputation for complaining, so if laugh therapy will work with them, it will work anywhere." His goal is helping people give a higher priority to humor in everyday life. He says, "Jokes are fine, but the humorous events of everyday life are better medicine."

I read about Dr. Ljungdahl in Steve Simms' book *Mindrobics: How to Be Happy for the Rest of Your Life*. Simms explains that for thirteen weeks Ljungdahl meets with his patients as they review books, comedy records, and humorous videos. (Yes, he does see the value of "jokes.") But then for homework, he asks patients to keep a journal of funny happenings they observe. They are to rank them on a one-to-five scale from barely funny to hilarious. In the course of the therapy, all the patients experienced a reduction in their levels of pain. Their immune systems improved, as well as the overall quality of their lives.

Dr. Ljungdahl concludes by saying, "The humor perspective is a way of getting distance from your problems. Since every person has a sense of humor and every child laughs, it's not so much learning something new as it is regaining what you once had." Does that sound familiar to you? Can you hear Jesus saying that we must "receive the kingdom of God like a little child" (Luke 18:17)?

Have you ever thought about the possibility of Jesus laughing. I have a picture on my desk of Jesus laughing. I love that picture. Can you imagine what his laugh might have sounded like. Do you think he was a snorter or a guffawer? Jo Berry says, in her book *Managing Your Life and Time*, "I used to puzzle over why the Holy Spirit didn't direct the authors of the Gospels to write, 'Jesus laughed,' as well as 'Jesus wept.' I've decided the reason is because it's so obvious that the Lord would laugh. It goes without saying. . . . Jesus was human, as well as divine, so of course He laughed. He enjoyed life, relished close friendships, and took great pleasure in being with children."

She reminds us that the classic "Westminster Confession of Faith declares it is our Christian duty to enjoy God."

And Martin Luther once said, "It is pleasing to God whenever you rejoice or laugh from the bottom of your heart." Is this sinking in yet? Do you get my point? God created you to laugh.

Laughter Therapy

Since I am a comedian, it should come as no surprise that I would write a chapter specifically about laughter. But all comedy aside, laughter should be a big part of your life. Because laughter is an incredible medicine created in us by God. No matter how much your heart may be hurting in this season of life or how tense and anxious you may be on this particular day, I want you to just try to find a little piece of life that gives you the hope of a chuckle.

I am well aware of the paradox that comes along with laughter: On one hand, healing takes time; it is a process that cannot be forced or rushed, and yet I've repeatedly seen that laughter does its healing work as we allow it to—in no time at all. Laughter may release endorphins that help you feel better, but it also is sometimes the key that will open the door of your heart. I suggest you engage in a bit of your own laughter therapy. And here are some ideas of how to get started.

1. Have lunch—or just go for a walk—with several people whose humor you appreciate, people who have made you laugh in the past. (I'm available on Tuesdays!) It's not clear why, but laughter is contagious. One study shows that gathered groups laugh thirty times as often as people who are alone. And people laugh more at television shows with laugh tracks than at the same shows without the canned laughter. My maternal grandfather, Thaddeus M. Whalen, better known as Papaw, made our whole family laugh. (He was extremely contagious.) Every time we would drive down his road, we'd pass by a certain old crooked oak that would prompt a story; every time we would drive past the diner where he had met Nanny (my grandmother), there would be another story.

And Papaw, maybe unlike most storytellers, would always *begin* his stories with laughter—he would start laughing long before "Once upon a time . . ." And his laugh always started as a light chuckle; then it would spill over and spread about the room like a bag of popcorn that just wouldn't stop popping. The stories would never change. We'd heard them over and over. But we'd laugh anyway—because Papaw was laughing. It was contagious. I don't think we were laughing at the old jokes. We were laughing with his laughter.

2. Go to the ballpark and watch six-year-olds play T-ball. Their shirts and pants barely fit. All the hats are too big for their tiny heads. And when someone hits a ball, everyone (all twenty-three defense players) chases after it, pounces on it, wrestles for it, and when someone finally pulls free, he will hold it high like a trophy and then fling it as hard as he can in whatever direction he happens to have come up for air. And if the ball should land in the grass again, the whole gang picks up and stampedes for a second time (and even a third if necessary). But the kids seem to love to play the game that way. On the way home after many games, Zach would be drinking his free drink and licking the powders from a grape Pixie Stix while asking, "Hey! Did we win?"

3. *Rent* The Ghost and Mr. Chicken, *starring Don Knotts.* (CAUTION: THIS MOVIE IS NOT RECOMMENDED FOR EXPECTANT MOTHERS.) You see, one night David and I went over to Alison and her husband's home to eat oatmeal-raisin cookies and watch this movie. About halfway through, right after Don Knotts had spent the night in the "haunted house" and was running about bug-eyed and screaming, "Shears in the throat! Shears in the throat!" Alison went into labor. (Have you ever seen anyone laugh and scream at the same time?) We had to pause the VCR and head to the hospital. (And I'm certain it was not very polite of us to be laughing about this movie constantly while she was in so much pain.)

4. *Watch Andy Griffith reruns.* Especially look for the episodes with Floyd.

5. *Skip down a sidewalk.* Okay, maybe not. But do something out of the ordinary. Lose your inhibitions once in a while and swing from the old tire swing one more time.

6. *Tell someone you like and trust about one hilariously wonderful memory of yours.* Surely you have one, somewhere in there. Now, I understand if you're overwhelmed with grief, this may be hard. You may cry before you get to the laughter. Here's where you may walk through the grim before you get to the grin. But just try it. Let the emotions roll down like a river.

I recently read an article about Bill Cosby and a funny moment that happened at his son's funeral. Cosby's daughter had laid a fishing pole in the casket with her brother, Ennis. Cosby said, "He's going to heaven, and up there they have the finest fishing poles ever. Don't embarrass him by making him drag that old thing up there."

7. *Sing in the shower.* Sing loudly enough for your dog to hear (and if you don't have one, then sing loudly enough for your neighbor's dog to hear). And so as not to forget why you are singing, try "This is the day, that the Lord hath made."

8. *Clip out funny comics or church bulletin bloopers and post them in places you go often.* Jan Smith works in my office to keep all the details of my life pasted together. But she also clips hilarious cartoons from magazines and sends them to me, and I stick them to my refrigerator door with magnets. Sometimes when I'm rushing around, trying to get the kids ready and off to school (and I should be screaming for the tenth time "You're going to be late!"), I'll find myself chuckling at Blondie trying to get Dagwood ready for work. Instead of screaming, I just smile and say, "That's okay, Zach. We all trip from time to time and spill our eggs all over the living room floor." (Lucky for Zach!)

Do you get the picture? Are you seeking out a laugh or two? Work at it! If you do, I think eventually you'll be like me. The medicine will work its wonder. The endorphins will flow, your heart will open, and comfort (in the form of the Spirit) will enter.

Sometimes while I'm sitting on a plane, I will think of something that made me laugh once before, and I laugh again. And then again on another day, maybe when I'm walking through a grocery store or filling the dishwasher.

Yes, I collect laughs like others collect marbles or butterflies. I mean that in two ways. I collect the sounds of laughter. I also collect the memories that make for repeated laughter. It works like this. On a particularly happy day author Henri Nouwen wrote in his journal that became known as *The Genesee Diary*: "I hope that the day will come when the memory of my present joy will give me the strength to keep giving even when loneliness gnaws at my heart."

He wanted "the memory of my present joy" to help him get through some future bleak days (like Sarah). He knew the storm clouds would return. They always do.

Maybe you can start your own collection of laughs. This very day you can do something that will add to your permanent collection of pleasant, laugh-worthy memories.

Remember, there is no childproof cap on this bottle. And there are unlimited refills. So when was the last time you had a good laugh? When was the last time you got those old endorphins flowing? It's time to take your medicine.

Eleven

Breast Cancer, No Laughing Matter, But . . .

They that wait upon the LORD shall renew their strength; they shall mount up with wings as eagles; they shall run, and not be weary; and they shall walk, and not faint.

Isaiah 40:31 KJV

I leaned against the wall of the small examining room. Dr. Laura Dunbar greeted us in her calm, kind voice, but the furrow across her eyebrows gave me every indication that she did not have good news.

A few days earlier, on Thanksgiving Day, 1994, we were washing the dishes after a giant dinner when Mother nonchalantly mentioned to Doris and me that she had an "annoying" lump on her right breast.

"How long has it been there, Mom?" I asked.

"Oh, about six months or so."

So much for early detection. She had just simply (mis)diagnosed it herself and waited for it to go away. It never did go away, so now she sat on the examining table, nervously knitting her fingers together. I placed my arm across her shoulders, and she reached up to pat my hand.

Dr. Dunbar took a deep breath and then reported to us some early test results: "Virginia, it doesn't look real good." She told us we needed to schedule surgery as soon as possible. During the surgery, she explained, they would conduct a biopsy and determine if the lump was benign or not. If not, then she would proceed with a radical mastectomy and then check the lymph nodes to see if they had been affected.

But there was also another concern—Mother's asthma. Mother has had asthma since birth, and with less than forty-percent use of her lungs, the doctors were quite concerned about putting her under a heavy anesthetic for her impending surgery. And because her case was so extreme, Dr. Dunbar set up a series of tests to see exactly what her lungs and heart could tolerate.

So many words that day carved themselves into my thoughts: *biopsy, radical mastectomy, lymph nodes.*

Over the next few days we visited the lung specialist and the heart doctor. Yet with the growing concern about the operation, Mother never lost her sense of humor.

Even her oncologist, Dr. Anthony Melluch, noticed my mother's unbelievable, positive attitude. He had ordered an extra test or two to be run on Mother's heart. (Nothing like a good stress test to stress you out!) At the end of that long day, Dr. Tony burst through the waiting room door with a folder full of graphs and charts. "Wow, Virginia," he said, flipping through pages, "looks like you have a good heart!" I could have told him that without all those tests. She grinned at him and without skipping a beat (no pun intended) said, "Why, thank you, honey. Aren't you a sweet boy!?"

The day came for Mother's surgery. Dr. Dunbar stopped by the room to talk with Mike, Mom, and me a few minutes before Mom was wheeled away. She said they should know something— whether to proceed with the longer surgery or not—just a few moments into the operation. A nurse would show us where we could wait (and pray), and we thanked her for her kindness. Before she could leave, Mike asked her if she would like to stay and have a word of prayer with us. She raised her eyebrows, considered the request, and with a smile said, "I would love to."

As Mike prayed, tears filled my eyes. I didn't want Mom to see how worried I was. Mike and I had agreed to be optimistic before Mom, so as soon as Mike said amen, I did what I usually do: stand-up comedy.

"Hey, Doc. You wanna hear our top ten list of things you don't want to hear during breast surgery?! Number 10: Hand me those scissors over there on the floor. Number 9: Boy, do I have a hangover!"

The room brightened a little as we added more to the list. A nurse in the room politely covered her mouth. (Maybe it is unprofessional to guffaw over your patient as you check her blood pressure—I don't know.)

"Number 3: Can I borrow your glasses? I left mine at home. Number 2: I haven't done this procedure since med school! And the Number 1 thing you don't want to hear during your mastectomy: Was that the right breast or the left breast we were supposed to remove?"

We were all laughing, especially Mother! And best of all, this little laugh seemed to make the time pass easier. As they wheeled her into the elevator I said, "Mom, can I have your bra if you're not going to use it anymore!?" (Okay, so I'm not always funny!) Still, Mom laughed and that felt good.

(I have a feeling that laughter in a "no laughing zone" has been going on for a long, long time. There had to be incidents when God must have watched his creation unfold and sometimes just sat back and grinned, even chuckled out loud. When did Adam find out that bees sting? Better yet, *how* did Adam find out that bees sting? How did Eve learn that a cactus does not make for a very good seat cushion? You know God must have had some great laughs!)

After Mom's surgery, while she was still sleeping off the anesthetic, my brother and I began to toss around some ideas about how to lift her spirits before she had to hear the news of what they had found during her surgery. I thought I had come up with the perfect comic relief. I thought if Mom could just wake up looking like Dolly Parton—that would take the sting away from hearing about the radical mastectomy, the lymph nodes removed, the biopsy that had proved positive, and the "C" word—*cancer*.

There. I'd said it. Cancer. I really hate that word. The word itself has a stench that causes me to choke. It is dark and ominous. It evokes images of scaly little bugs scurrying across slick floors, stealing away the supplies from the storehouse one grain at a time—so fast, so slick that they can't be squashed. (I told you I really hate that word!)

But with all those dark images in my mind, I still wanted to fill some balloons and lay them across Mom's chest. I just couldn't get the rest of the family to go along with it. (Some people just have no sense of humor!)

Okay, maybe I have a few more things to learn about laughing at the wrong time. But at least I have found peace in knowing that my laughter now is flowing from the right place. (At least I didn't say something like, "See, we're dropping like flies.") Don't get me wrong. I know there are days when laughing seems impossible. And one may never get to the place where every day is a victory day. Even now there are earthly reminders that cause me to stop and frown and shed a tear—events, holidays, places that cause me to reflect on what's missing or who's absent from my life. But God's grace and mercy extends far beyond a depressing moment.

And I also struggle for other people, people in my life who are walking through some of those long, trying days within God's time clock. I want so badly to speed up the minutes for them—to create an expanse of time so the grief won't be so pointed, to burn the days away so long-term financial goals can be met, to get those long, character-building, seed-planting, learning experiences behind us so happiness can begin. But through Mom's ordeal, I learned even more about God's incredible timing.

Time Drags On

The weeks and the months after Mom's surgery seemed to move the slowest. Mother had to have over ten chemotherapy sessions, a regimen customized for her by Dr. Tony Melluch and Johns Hopkins University. This regimen was the strongest amount of chemotherapy that her body could possibly tolerate. But with nineteen lymph nodes removed and seventeen of them testing positive for cancer, she needed every dose. Dr. Tony explained how each session would build on the other—a cumulative effect—and therefore each treatment must be administered carefully. They would monitor her blood count; if the white count dropped too low, infection could kill her. Dr. Tony assured us that this process was going to be slow and tedious.

I went every time she had a treatment and watched the IV drip its healing solution so slowly. I was so tempted to slide the little drip indicator to Super Drip to hurry things along.

Week after week after week. The process was so slow. Even the thirty-mile drive to the hospital seemed to take so long. (Mom said I was driving too fast.) And then the radiation treatments—I even offered to clean the lenses of the radiation cameras because everything seemed to be working so slowly.

Some days she would weep. Some days she would be so physically sick and weak—she would be disoriented. Some days she would ache. Why couldn't God just zap her well and let us carry on as we had before? But it seemed the most I could do was to give her her medicine, make her comfortable, and make her laugh.

Of course, Mom had heard all my "work," so to make her laugh with my stories was not easy. But she has always been able to laugh by watching the faces of those who are listening to my stories for the first time. Because I knew this (and because I know she's a bit proud of her little girl!), I loaded Mom up with videos—videos of me on different TV shows—with Pat Boone on his gospel show and with Terry Meeuwsen of *The 700 Club*, or the Grand Ole Opry, and especially some of those Bill Gaither videos. And then whenever Mom would have someone over (or if anyone happened to drop in trying to sell water purifiers or magazines), she would offer the most comfortable chair right in front of the television and start the VCR. And as her guests would watch me, she would be watching them. They would laugh; she would laugh. The endorphins would flow, and Mother would grow stronger.

And every day I was reminded that, try as I might, I could not make the clock tick faster. I am closer to forty than thirty (something I'd rather you wouldn't spread around), and I still need to be reminded that God is in control, and I'm not. (That's a relief!)

Not too long ago, someone suggested I set my clock ahead ten minutes. "That way you'll never be late," he said. This was my one chance to speed up the clock and what did I do? I kept reminding myself that the clock was ten minutes fast, and I still wound up late everywhere I went. (I don't have time or space to relate my woes with time zone changes. And don't even get me started on daylight savings time.)

I took my concerns about the slow passing of time to one of my pastors. At first, Pastor Phillip Jackson nodded as if he really understood and was going to sympathize with my position. Softly he spoke. "Oh my, so we are a little God now, are we!?" That hurt, but I deserved it. Actually, this sage advice came on about my fifth pastoral counseling visit where I showed up as Chonda the Incredible Watchmaker. "Chonda, is that your job?" Pastor Phillip asked. (I believe he was being rhetorical.) "Is that your calling? I don't think so! Can you relax and let God take care of this?"

He's absolutely right! I cannot rush God's work in myself much less in and for someone I love. No matter how much I think I've learned! No matter how funny I try to be or how quickly I want time to fly by, I know that I must rest in the good timing of the One who can take care of all problems—when the time is "right." His time.

Phillips Brooks once said, "I believe I have spent half my life waiting for God to catch up with me."

If that's how you feel, catch a load of this, found in God's Word:

> Since ancient times no one has heard,
> no ear has perceived,
> no eye has seen any God besides you,
> who acts on behalf of those who wait for him. (Isaiah 64:4)

And this:

> The LORD longs to be gracious to you;
> he rises to show you compassion.
> For the LORD is a God of justice.
> Blessed are all who wait for him! (Isaiah 30:18)

How to Make Time Fly

Waiting is tough. But while you wait, "The Lord longs to be gracious to you." And to those you love. Can you reach out and grasp that? If not, try this on those slow-moving days toward healing—to your "victory days." Try memorizing and living out this verse: "Give thanks in all circumstances, for this is God's will for you in Christ Jesus" (1 Thessalonians 5:18). You see, it doesn't say, "Always FEEL thankful." That would be tough. It is not always a matter of emotions, but a matter of faith in and obedience to the God who knows the beginning and the end.

And in those long days of waiting for healing, waiting for God's will to be done, how did Mother pass her time? Praising him, of course. I've watched my mother praise God right there in her living room by the light of her TV screen, hooked up to her chemo IV—weeping and praying and praising.

Mother, in her living room or on the highway, has taught me what no watchmaker ever could: how to make time fly. For example, on one of those trips to the heart doctor, my mother began what was quickly becoming a routine speech: "We're going to beat this thing. Isn't God so good? Let's just praise him for the flowers in the field today!" I was fighting back the tears. (I guess my attitude in the midst of crisis was not as angelic as Mother's!) Just as a tear began to course down my face, she did it! She made me laugh!

Right after *Oh, isn't this a beautiful world God has created?* and while I was waiting to hear, *I know his presence is so real today, darling,* a car swerved in front of us, causing me to brake and swerve to the shoulder of the highway.

Without the slightest pause, Mother's tone shifted from angelic to something that could have come from a late night horror movie: "Look at that nut case, honey! Just lay on your horn! That stupid man shouldn't even be driving!"

I lost it. So much for angelic thoughts. Her sense of humor is great. And what a sense of timing!

We laughed all the way to town. And I paid particular attention to Mother's laugh, one colored with an air of peace. I saved that laugh for my collection. It happens to be one that I sometimes take out and hold to the light and marvel that it can even exist.

You see, sometimes I choose to hang on to the impending doom of the moment or I try to rush the punch line. Mother, on the other hand, has chosen to simply relax, hold on to her purse, and smile at the flowers in the fields. She is content and willing to wait upon God's timing. (She also knows that time flies when you're having fun! Why didn't *I* think of that?) Will she never stop teaching me? Probably not!

Twelve

Knock, Knock. Who's There?

Do not forget to entertain strangers, for by so doing some people
have entertained angels without knowing it.

Hebrews 13:2

Not long after Mother's mastectomy, we brought home a ton of brochures and information from the American Cancer Society. We found all sorts of information about wigs, financial assistance, support groups, and prostheses. Yes, prostheses. Mom made an appointment and one day a health care worker came to her house for the task of fitting her for a prosthetic bra. She learned that this kind woman had been through the very same surgery as she had, and it was comforting to Mother to be able to ask all kinds of questions in the privacy of her own home. But there was probably too much time for Mother to ask her questions. Because at 4:30 that afternoon *my* doorbell rang.

I answered the door to discover a woman in a white medical-type coat standing there. She introduced herself and handed me her card and began to tell me how much she had enjoyed the day with my mother. (Uh-oh!) They had talked about everything. (Uh-oh!) And, of course, Mother had shown her my latest comedy video and some clips from the Opry, and "she just felt like she knew me now." (Uh-oh!) She told me that she'd had a nice bra-fitting session with my mother and that this new bra should help her to feel good about her figure again.

Then, with very little pause, she added, "And your mother told me you've always been self-conscious about being so small, and she thought I should stop by here and show you what is available." She patted her black case and smiled. "She thought you might want to use one of these."

I was tempted. But after I convinced the kind saleswoman that I was content with my size, we laughed.

Afterward, I was able to sit down with this woman and ask some tough questions about Mother's cancer and what we could expect in the months ahead. I asked her about the statistics with this kind of cancer. The survival rate. Is this hereditary? Should I have a mammogram regularly? Will my mother die?

I knew she had sensed my mother's incredible attitude. (And she knew Mom had a good, strong heart.) "A positive attitude is ninety percent of the battle," she said. "So I think your mother's going to make it through this just fine." I really needed that woman that day—not what she was selling, but her words of encouragement.

Born with a Laugh

Sometimes God sends just the right person, with just the right words, at just the right time to give you the added assurance you are longing for. Such was the case during another occasion—when Zachary was born.

But first let me tell you a brief version of Chera Kay's birth. The night Chera Kay was born, I woke David up and said (for the third time—have I told you that David is, well, a little slow?), "It really is time, honey. I think my water just broke." I don't know if it was the third punch on his arm, or the warm sensation across the quilt, but he finally jumped up, rushed through the house, got the packed suitcase, helped me slip my robe on, and escorted me out the door and into the front seat of the car. As he slipped under the wheel, I said, "The car keys are in your pants pocket. (Hint.) The pants pocket still hanging on the end of the bed. (Another hint.) The ones you need to put on *before* we go to the hospital."

This was my first child. I had heard horror stories of how the first one usually takes a lot longer, twenty to thirty hours of labor sometimes. But with Chera we got to the hospital at 10 that night and at 2:15 A.M. she was born.

In the delivery room the doctor said, "One more push and this one will be out."

David, with a tone of panic in his voice, said, "There's not more than one, is there?"

I raised up to laugh. Then Dr. Baer chuckled. "Whoa! Don't laugh too hard or this little one will land on the floor!"

I couldn't help it. Dr. Baer made a fine catch, and Chera Kay was born with a laugh. (Is that something like poetic justice for a comedian?)

When Chera Kay was midway through her terrible twos, David and I decided that it was time we had another baby. We thought the first one had turned out pretty well. "We're on a roll here! How hard can it be?" Three years apart sounded like a nice round, odd number with minimal overlapping—diapers, college. Yes, three years apart would be testament of good timing. But we weren't exactly in charge.

Having Your Baby

Chera Kay was almost six years old when Zachary was born. (So much for *our* timing!)

It was a tough pregnancy. I battled full-blown gestational diabetes, premature labor, and all-around misery! (Did you know you can eat all the cabbage in the world and it won't change your blood sugar? Yeah, but who wants to!) The only good timing David and I could witness was the routine we had established whenever the labor pains would start: call the doctor, start timing the contractions, rush to the hospital to get the IV started that would administer the medication that would stop the labor. We'd run through this routine every few weeks like clockwork. We'd had a bit of practice with Chera Kay, so now we were old pros.

Six weeks before my due date, we began the routine again. David came home from work, and we went to the hospital. (It looked like another vending-machine dinner that night.) But a few moments after we got there, before the nurse could start the IV, my doctor walked in and said, "Well, what do you think?" (I thought that's what I was paying him to do!) A neonatal specialist had followed him into the room, and they began to measure me and to talk as if I were invisible. Finally, my obstetrician said, "Okay, let's go ahead and have this baby." They explained the risks involved in delivery now and the risks involved in waiting. Then before I hardly knew what was happening, I was being wheeled into an operating room.

"But we had arranged to have a birthing room," I protested. You know, nice furniture with doilies and draperies and a rocking chair to make you feel at home. But the nurse said no way. Such a high-risk birth would have to take place in the operating room—the cold and freezing operating room.

Two nurses lifted me onto a table—a freezing table. A tiny little glass box—an incubator—with tubes and wires connected to it was parked in one corner of the room. A nurse and doctor stood ready to whisk the baby into intensive care if need be. David, covered from head to toe in green surgical clothes, stood by the left side of my head. All I could see of the real him were his eyes—looking larger than usual—peering out between his mask and "shower" cap.

The labor pains got worse very quickly, and they gave me an epidural (one of God's greatest gifts to women!). I don't know whose fault it was but the epidural only worked on one side. "Give me another one!" I begged.

"No. It's too late. It's almost time," the doctor said. "You may not feel much, if anything, on your right side," he added, "but the left side will feel as if you are having Zachary naturally."

Believe me there is nothing natural about the screams of childbirth. The person I believed to be David was really a robot programmed to say "Are you all right? Are you all right?" every five seconds.

Fortunately, after less than five hours of labor, Zachary was born. He cried. He looked perfect. He looked just like Chera Kay had looked five years earlier (in the face at least). They weighed Zachary, cleaned him up, wrapped him in a blanket, and then a nurse who had been there the whole time cradled him in her arms and took him away—to the nursery I was told. David—still the green giant—gave me a kiss through his mask, grabbed the video camera, and left.

My mother and our friends, the Hunts, joined David. They all goo-gooed and tapped on the nursery window while the nurses fussed over the giant preemie that weighed in at over six pounds. David shot some video through the nursery window. Sometimes we sit and play it back and crack up at everyone's comments: "Oh, I think he looks like David's daddy." "Oh no, he's the spitting image of Charlotta." "Well, you know he has a little bit of Papaw Whalen's chin." It was like a contest, with the latest guess always the winner. Before long they were naming people who weren't related to either one of us!

On the herky-jerky video, as I can hear the voices making a fuss about Zachary, I see my baby suddenly change: His chest laboring for every breath. His face turning from pink to red to purple. The voices eerily stop. Then I hear my mother's voice: "Oh my, I think something is wrong. I'm glad Chonda can't see this." A nurse steps in front of the camera and quickly pulls the curtain closed.

Back in the recovery room I was dozing but growing impatient. I knew everyone was down the hall making a fuss over the baby and I couldn't wait to hold him and count his toes. No more than an hour after Chera Kay was born, I had been able to rock her and to nurse her. I couldn't imagine what was taking so long.

Finally, David and Mother walked in. He lifted my hand to his face and kissed my fingers. (That was the only thing that didn't hurt!) The doctor followed them in and explained that Zachary was in an oxygen tent and doing okay. But they thought he should stay put in the nursery for a while. If I settled into my own room and got some rest, then I could see him. The family went home to get some sleep.

Message from Heaven

I don't know how long I had been asleep when Dr. Rojas, a neonatal specialist, tapped me on the shoulder. "Mrs. Pierce. Mrs.

Pierce I need to talk to you." He was a tall dark-headed, thin man. He looked tired. He held a clipboard in his hand and a pen. "Your son has taken a turn for the worse . . ." he said ominously.

He needed my signature to treat the baby immediately. They had placed him on a respirator and needed to move him to the neonatal care unit. "He's critical, but we're not worried yet." (To a mother, is that mumbo jumbo or what?) "We treat premature babies at all stages and we have seen some great miracles take place."

"Premature? Six or seven weeks early, yes, but I thought he weighed six pounds!"

He explained that in this case birth weight had nothing to do with his gestation development. "With your diabetes, he would have probably weighed ten or eleven pounds at full term; we call them 'sugar babies.' Your son's lungs aren't developed very well. He's not getting enough oxygen to his brain. And . . . because of your negative blood type, we need to give him a complete blood transfusion. There are a few more minor things, but these need immediate attention."

Tears welled up in my eyes. David isn't here, and I'm signing papers to allow a handful of strangers to take care of my baby, and I haven't even had the chance to hold him yet.

Dr. Rojas realized my pain and had some unforgettable words: "Mrs. Pierce, this was your son's day to come into this world. This is his time. We just need to help his body do a little catching up now." I signed the papers and he left—to get busy.

It was after 2 A.M., but I called David anyway and explained as best I could what was happening. He called Mother. And Mother called the rest of the world! But I got to my brother first. It was about three o'clock in the morning when I called him long distance, giving him details, asking for prayer. If this was Zachary's time to come into this world, then this was the time to surround him with prayer.

After I talked with Mike, I tried to sleep, but that was impossible. So just before five, I staggered out of bed, slipped on my robe, walked to the nurses' station, and asked someone to escort me to my son. (I wanted to surround him with my arms as well.) The nurse offered a wheelchair. I said I wanted to walk. In the elevator she told me about the great number of babies who have been born so early but are now healthy, older kids. She told me all about Dr. Rojas and his excellent reputation. "He is an expert in this field, really. You can relax." I wish I could remember her name. She was a true bright spot in that dark night.

We stepped out of the elevator. I followed the nurse who pushed open a huge metal door that said STOP! DO NOT ENTER WITHOUT PERMISSION. Once inside I had to scrub down and put on the same green surgical clothes—gloves, booties, shower cap, and mask—that I had seen David in earlier. All this green garb simply to be able to look at my baby!

We stepped into a room noisy with the sounds of whirling air pumps and beeping electronic monitors. Little glass boxes like the one I had seen in the delivery room contained the tiniest human beings I had ever seen, most of them no bigger than my hand, all hooked up to tubes and IVs. Oxygen tanks grouped in twos and threes stood like steely guards at their heads and feet. And everywhere there were nurses—lots of nurses, stroking, feeding, burping, loving, even singing to the tiny, naked infants.

Soft music played, but I could barely hear it over the machines. I followed my guide, and we wove through the maze until she pointed. "There he is," she said. "There's your little buddy."

His eyes were bandaged. A skinny, ice-blue tube came out of his nose; a dark red one extended from his foot. The transfusion would take hours, I had been told. That's what was going on now. He was so still, lifeless. Just before a tear could spill out of my eye, a nurse behind me said, "Don't worry, he's just sleeping right now. Earlier he was kicking and screaming. Your son has a temper and doesn't want to be disturbed when he's sleeping! You can touch him if you want to."

I stuck my hand into the incubator's small round porthole fitted with a rubber glove. I had once seen someone on TV handle moon rocks like this. I pushed my hand deep into the glove so I could feel his skin as best as I could through the protective latex. He budged a bit, wiggled a finger, and grunted. I wanted so badly to hold him.

The doctor had entered the room and came over. "I can just about give you a list of events that will take place before your son leaves this room," he told me. "First, his blood oxygen count will get better. We'll keep checking his bilirubin, and eventually we will wean him off of the respirator. We will do a few tests to check for brain damage, but your son is responding very well to touch and sound. He will probably still need some more blood, so if it will ease your mind, you can check to see if some family members would like to donate. We will keep a close watch on his eyes as well as signs of any kidney failure. . . . The list may vary a bit, but believe me, he's in the right place, and we are prepared for much worse. It is a slow process, but your son will go home soon. It just takes time."

I stood by the incubator for a few more minutes before I noticed a little Post-it note that someone had stuck near the top:

Message for Baby Pierce received at 3:29 A.M.:

"Someone is praying for you at this time in your new life. We love you."

Amazing! This simple message on the little square of yellow brought such peace to me! Somewhere out there someone was awake and praying for my brand-new son. (If you possess Post-it notes, you have the potential to be a great encourager—don't squander your opportunities.) I stayed by my son's little glass house as long as I could, stroking his tiny face, bending and unbending his tiny fingers. Then I shuffled back to my room to rest and to wait.

A few hours later, Michael called to check on his new nephew. I thanked him for sending the note. "What note?"

I seemed to get that response from everyone I asked. (Do angels use Post-it notes?)

My doctor allowed me to stay in the hospital an extra day to "watch my blood sugar." I think he was just a softy when it came to mothers who have to leave the hospital without their newborns.

When it was time to go, David pulled the car up to the curb, and I slipped out of the wheelchair and into the front seat. Aware of our new—and very empty—car seat, we drove home mostly in silence. I reached over and turned on the radio just as a popular song was playing: "Somewhere out there . . . someone's thinking of you. . . ." I started sobbing. David turned the radio off and said, "It's a just a dumb song, honey! Don't let it upset you."

Yes, someone was thinking of Zachary—and not just David and me. Others from Ohio, others from Tennessee and—if Mom had anything to do with it—others from about three or four different states were all thinking and praying for Zachary, just like the words on the Post-it note had said. We were collectively surrounding him with our prayers.

Zachary weighed less than five pounds and was more than ten days old when we finally brought him home. He amazed all of the nurses and doctors at how well he had responded. As the doctor had assured us, he was a normal, healthy baby boy—with a temper.

Perfect Timing

When I think of this story, I am so grateful for the words spoken—by the nurse in the elevator, by the doctor at my bedside, and in the note sent—just at the right time.

Chuck Swindoll says in his book *The Finishing Touch*, "All of us need encouragement. All of us need somebody to believe in us. To reassure and reinforce us. To help us pick up the pieces and go on. To provide us with increased determination in spite of the odds. We all need encouragement. . . . and we all need to be encouragers."

Hebrews 10:24–25 reminds us, "And let us consider how we may spur one another on toward love and good deeds. Let us not give up meeting together, as some are in the habit of doing, but let us encourage one another—and all the more as you see the Day approaching." Could it be the author of Hebrews had discovered a few encouraging messengers in his life?

There are so many potential healing moments in our lives, ministered through the gift of someone's encouraging word or touch, life-changing moments. However, all too often we miss them because we are too busy, preoccupied with our own misery or fear, preoccupied with the business of life; we fail to stop long enough to hear him speak through the most unlikely servants in the most unlikely places in the most unlikely ways.

Looking back on my life, I can see countless times when God sent messengers of hope and comfort to me. A neighbor who fixed an extra casserole for our supper or vacuumed the living room before unexpected guests arrived. A lady in a gingham dress and a straw hat with a price tag dangling down. A boss who asked, "Would you be interested in impersonating Minnie Pearl and telling a few jokes?" A funny story that brought a reprieve from a busy day. A prosthetic bra saleswoman! An assuring Post-it note.

The timing of the message—as always when God is involved—was incredible and perfect. And it will be tomorrow too. The question is, are we listening for him?

Thirteen

Amazing Goats, Grace, and Chickens

Whatever you have learned or received or heard from me, or seen in me—put
it into practice. And the God of peace will be with you.
Philippians 4:9

You can experience the scenic rolling hills of Ashland City, Tennessee, from the comforts of your car. But if you want to fully appreciate the lush greenery of the woodlands, the undulation of the highway, or the fishy, muddy smell of the river—you've got to see the sights from beneath a helmet while riding on a motorcycle. That's right, a motorcycle! I hesitate to even write this chapter because until now I've been fairly successful at keeping my own church version of "Born to Be Wild" a secret. But the truth is, I've always loved motorcycles.

My dad, the fix-it man, was very mechanical and always seemed to be tinkering with an old car. And then there was his street bike, a CB125 Honda. It wasn't a big bike or extremely powerful. We had the greatest fun riding around the yard with Dad, doing our stunts. (Move over Evel Knievel!) Cheralyn would stand on the seat behind Dad and hang on, and I would ride on his shoulders. (Kids, never try this at home!) And then Dad would ride around and around in circles in the backyard until Mom would fuss at him enough to make him stop. (Mom just wasn't cut out to be a biker!) Wow, that was fun! That's when I fell in love with motorcycles. To me they represented freedom—and just the right thing to get Mom going!

We moved from the beach to the little town of Ashland City when I was in the tenth grade. Mike and Charlotta were in college in Nashville about twenty-five miles away. This is when Mike got a dirt bike (lucky!). That's also when we discovered the best way to enjoy the scenic, rolling hills around our new hometown was on a bike. Sometimes Charlotta's and Mike's college friends would stay over for Sunday dinner, and we would take turns taking long rides down the winding road next to the Cumberland River.

Goats and Chickens

One afternoon Ricky Morris, a good friend of Charlotta's, and I had been riding along for a while. It was great. I hung on to Ricky and peeped around his shoulders. The wind was in my hair. The bugs were in my teeth (just kidding!). The roar (whine) of the engine was in my ears. And freedom seemed to whip all around me. Suddenly, without warning, the motorcycle began to cough and sputter and then it died. Ricky coasted to the side of the road and we started tapping the gauges. "It can't be out of gas," he said. "The gauge says it still has half a tank." (I wouldn't learn the secret of carburetors for some time.)

He kept tapping, but I wasn't looking at the gas gauge anymore. "Ah, Rick . . . ah, Ricky." The rest of the words seemed to get stuck in my throat. "There are . . . goats. Big goats. Ricky, RUN! There are goats chasing us!" Never had the wildlife at Myrtle Beach attacked us. But here in Tennessee we found ourselves running from a herd of billy goats.

We pushed the bike to the top of the hill, panting and sweating, the sound of hoofbeats moving closer. I was wondering how to stop charging goats. *Maybe we'll go over a bridge and a troll will eat them*, I thought. At the top of the hill we jumped on the bike. Ricky kicked at the gear shift and miraculously the bike started just as this huge billy goat nudged the back of my seat. I guess freedom has its price.

Later that same year, when I was fifteen, Dad took me down to the county courthouse, and I applied for a motorcycle license of my very own. (I guess, in his eyes, since I had passed the goat test, I was qualified.) But really I think Mom and Dad were being so cool about my getting my own license because neither of them liked getting up at 4:30 in the morning to drive me to work—at Shirley's Bakery.

Shirley's Bakery—which was really more like a diner—was the hot spot in our little town. And at 5:00 every morning I served grits and eggs. Later in the day I would decorate a few birthday cakes before heading off to school on Dad's Honda (the mean CB125). The bike wasn't a very big one—for Dad—but for me it was just big enough that whenever it would fall over at school, I would have to ask one of my teachers to help me set it up again. The kick starter was tough, especially since I only weighed seventy-eight pounds. (I believe it was designed to start with seventy-nine pounds.) I could have really used an automatic starter. It was during my Shirley's Bakery days that I earned the nickname—you guessed it—"Honda-Chonda"!

But I loved it!

It was better than another name I could have earned after another incident, this time involving some feathered friends. One Saturday morning, I was coming around a sharp curve in front of our church on my way to work at the diner. Just ahead I noticed a few chickens in the road pecking at the asphalt. (Did I mention Ashland City was a country town?) Being cautious and careful (or so I thought) I swerved all the way to the opposite edge of the highway.

(Did I mention that chickens are pretty stupid?—and quick?) I don't mean to be disrespectful to the entire chicken population, but let's face it—there is very little room for much brain matter in a chicken's head. They are just . . . stupid. And they panic.

I don't know if it was the roar (whine) of the motorcycle or the sight of something shiny rolling by that caught the rooster's eye, but . . . the bird flapped a couple of times, turned left then right and then ran right into me. Feathers flew. Some got tangled up in the bike's spokes and some in my clothes. First the front wheel went over the poor bird: *bump bump*. Then the back wheel: *bump bump*. The thrill of the open road would not be the same for me for a long, long time.

I walked into the back door at work. Most of the regulars were there, drinking coffee, eating grits. A half-dozen stopped in mid-bite and just stared at me. I guess there is something about running over a chicken that changes your appearance so much that you just can't hide it. Shirley glanced at her watch and asked me if everything was okay. "I was beginning to worry. Did you have bike trouble?"

I slipped off my helmet (a single feather twirled to the ground), and she caught a glance of my green face. "Ah, I had an accident."

She threw her arms around me, "Oh my goodness. Should I call your folks?"

"No. It's okay," I said. "I just feel terrible. I . . . I ran over a chicken."

"You did what?"

"I ran over a chicken."

Everyone in the diner burst out laughing, especially since Shirley had just scribbled the Special of the Day on the chalkboard above my head: Chicken Sandwich and Tater Tots.

My thrill for motorcycles was never quite the same after that. And I never ever thought my bike skills would come in handy again. I was wrong.

Bad News Gracefully

Nearly twenty years later I was speaking at a women's conference in Clarksville, Indiana. About three hundred ladies were sitting around banquet tables spread before me for the first session of that Saturday morning. I had not seen this many people gathered this early since my Shirley's Bakery days. (Sometimes I find it so hard to believe that so many people can actually move and talk—function—say nothing of laugh—before 9 A.M.) Like so many other times, I was watching the faces of those who were watching me—so appreciative of their attentiveness and of their smiles.

I don't know how other professional speakers do it, but for me I usually take the microphone and just jump in—with both feet! I usually have a pretty good idea where I'm going to land—where I want to go with a particular topic—but until I hear that first laugh,

I find myself holding my breath and hoping that someone is listening. (Of course, it doesn't hurt to plant a few friends in the crowd and pay them to laugh. Believe me, the thought has occurred!)

I was in the middle of a funny story about Old Brother Smith, the runner in my church who had a "run-in" with an amplifier, when I noticed a woman slip into the room through the back door. She stood for a while just inside the door, looking from one table to the next, searching for someone in particular. I didn't make much of it, tried not to look her way as I carried on. Brother Smith and I were on about the fourth lap around the room when the woman made her way, as discreetly as possible, to the head table, just in front of where I was standing and slipped a note to Sharon, the conference director. Part of me felt as if I were racing this lady with the note to the punch line. Some people turned to see, curious, but I kept telling my story. Someone probably drove in this morning and left their car lights on, I thought.

I kept an eye on Sharon as she read the note. She suddenly buried her face in her hands, and her shoulders began to shake. Something was very wrong. I worked hard to keep my concentration. Brother Smith was just about to trip over the speaker (just as he always does in this story), and then I would deliver the punch line, and there would be laughter, when Sharon stepped onto the platform and interrupted. I stepped back from the mike and listened intently. Her voice cracked as she read from the crumpled note in her hand: A group of women on their way to our event had been in an accident. One had been killed and another was seriously injured. The driver of the "other" car—a high school boy—had also been killed.

Beneath the collective gasps and moans and sighs of our gathered group, I sensed an awkward, uncomfortable silence. A few women who were from the same home church as the victims (someone later told me) turned ghastly white and quickly slipped out the door.

I had an emotional flashback as I looked at their faces. I remembered the day our phone had rung and Dad had told me that Charlotta had been killed. I remembered the shock and assault to my system as I listened to his words. I sat numb and silent at first, but quickly the sorrow overwhelmed us, and we cried together.

At a loss for words, Sharon handed the microphone back to me. There was no "jumping in" this time. I stared into a sea of sober, saddened faces. I was suddenly at the side of my big sister's casket again, watching her friends, my friends, nearly paralyzed with disbelief. It was not time for the punch line; it wouldn't be funny. I couldn't even remember the story I was telling. Instead, I looked at the group, took a deep breath, and said, "Let's pray."

I have discovered time and time again in my life that talking to God is always "timely." Discerning his Spirit and what he would have us learn and do in any situation is easiest when we simply ask him and then trust him to be on time. I always want to be prepared and strive to do my best in every performance, retreat, or encounter. But there are times when our best is not enough. We must trust the Holy Spirit to take our best and make it better. I want to be funny when the time is right. But I also want to be silent when the time is right, trusting God to fill in the gaps.

After prayer we sang a chorus or two, then God came. In the midst of it all, a sweet breeze of comfort soothed our hearts and calmed our confusion. Just in time.

The rest of the retreat was a reminder that in the tough times or the fun times, God is still God, and we need to draw ever closer to him. Before the day was over we could smile. We even managed a laugh.

But that's not the end of this story.

What a Hog!

Months later I was back in Indiana, on my way to Indianapolis. I hesitated to accept an invitation for dinner on my way through a small town, but the letter they had sent reminded me of our previously interrupted visit, and I knew in my heart that I needed to follow through with my newfound sisters in Christ. You see, this was the home church of the woman who'd died in that accident. The women inviting me were the ones who'd so suddenly left that retreat.

Now they wanted me to come to their church to share a quick devotional at a women's supper meeting. I had prayed for a long time about what I would say or do if I ever got an opportunity to meet with these women again. Now was the time.

My brother's wife, Doris, travels with me. Late that afternoon we pulled the van into the gravel parking lot of a beautiful little gray church. Doris was driving and was making her way to the visitor parking space when I first noticed it. "Stop! Stop!" I shouted to Doris. "Drop me off here!"

My jaw fell slack at the sight of it. Lots of chrome. Lots of metal. All Harley Davidson—right by the front door. I had a feeling my secret was about to be revealed.

A young man standing next to the bike slipped off his helmet and stuck out his hand to greet me. An older man stood beside him, with a helmet under his arm. A young woman who had come out to meet me introduced me to the handsome teenage boy. She explained that this was the son of the woman who had been killed on her way to the retreat. The man standing next to him was his father—her husband. They had been invited to join our women's supper. I also met the woman who had survived the accident. The reality of why I was here suddenly dulled the gleam of the motorcycle. What should I say?

For a moment I felt a tremendous load of responsibility. I had been praying about what I would say to this group of women. I had placed my trust in God to send the right words, but I hadn't expected this—standing face-to-face with a husband and a son who were grieving the loss of a wife and a mother. I took a deep breath and jumped in—with both feet again: "So, how 'bout it?" I said to the young man. "Gonna give me a ride?"

His eyebrows lifted. The parking lot "crowd" chuckled. I think they actually thought I was joking! (That happens a lot when you're a comedian.)

His father handed me his helmet, and I slipped it on my head. The sweetest grins fell across both their faces. I tightened my helmet and slid onto the "hog" (that's bike talk for Harley!). The young man revved up the engine, and the Harley lurched forward. The rear wheel spit gravel across the parking lot. We took a long ride all around town, laughing about the surprised looks on all those women's faces back at church.

"I think those ladies were pretty surprised you were taking a ride with me!" he said back over his shoulder. I asked him about his job, about his plans for college, and I reminded him how important a church family is during this time in his life. But mostly we just rode (without running over any wildlife). Before the end of our spin, I was thinking, *I'm gonna have to get me one of these.*

When we pulled back into the church driveway, his father was standing there, grinning and shaking his head in disbelief. I like to think it was his way of saying, "That's good. That's just what that boy needed." I put my arms around him and told them both how sorry I was for their loss.

Finally we all went into the fellowship hall and enjoyed a wonderful potluck supper. We sang a few choruses, prayed together, and even, yes, laughed. For a few moments our lives were linked together because of a death. Yet somehow, we were still able to make new memories—only this time tinted with joy and hope.

Everyone seemed so appreciative, but it was I who was the most grateful. Watching this sweet group of ladies extend their love to this grieving family was a beautiful expression of what the church is all about. As we said our good-byes, I told those two men how blessed they were to have a church family to rally around them.

We had met some folks and shared a meal. To some that is all that happened that night. But as Doris and I drove away (the memory of the growl of the Harley still fresh in my mind), we realized that we had just witnessed the church being the church—people helping, encouraging, and supporting one another.

Recycling Grace

I occasionally meet women—sometimes young, sometimes old—who seem to think they have virtually no "life experience" that God can use.

I wish I could have them sit in on our Leadership 2000 class at my church. Again and again Pastor Allen Jackson has told us that we are *all* ministers. He reminds us that we are one body with many parts. (Read 1 Corinthians 12.) And he also reminds us to "be yourself"; God has ordained your life and circumstances to minister hope to someone walking the same path you have been down before. Take a look at Paul's statement in 1 Corinthians 9:19–22: "Though I am free and belong to no man, I make myself a slave to everyone, to win as many as possible. To the Jews I became like a Jew, to win the Jews . . . To the weak I became weak, to win the weak. I have become all things to all men so that by all possible means I might save some."

Did you hear what I heard in that passage? God knows where you are and what you've been through—it is that very thing that he will use to "save some." He wants to use you—warts and all—because you are uniquely his and uniquely placed right where he needs you to be.

In his book *Healing for Damaged Emotions*, David Seamands refers to what he calls God's "recycling grace." Think in terms of a big recycling operation in which "garbage is turned into useful fuel for energy. In a similar way," says Seamonds, "God's recycling grace takes our infirmities, our damaged emotions, and the garbage of our lives and turns them from curses that cripple into means for growth and instruments to be used in His service."

I like Seamands's phrase "recycling grace." You see, God can use anything in our background to minister his grace to us and through us.

"But, I'm just a comedian," I've protested to my pastor. I keep telling people that, and I've even had to explain to the Lord on a few occasions that I "just do comedy." I tell funny stories, jokes, things that make people laugh. And no matter how much I try to explain my job qualifications to God, he reminds me that he uses the most unusable things sometimes. (Just read the story of Balaam's donkey in the Old Testament.) I guess that is God's way of reminding me that if he can use a donkey, then he can use a comedian!

Okay, okay, I do tell some "other" stories—the kind that aren't so funny, the kind laced with hurt and pain. I tell what I know, and I've known a bit of pain, but I'm no expert on pain. He reminds me that comedians can also comfort, encourage, and listen. Sometimes he sends someone my way—listening—and I wonder, *Why me? Why not a real expert? Why not a theologian or a psychiatrist?* All I know about hurt is that it comes, and it sure doesn't feel good. Believe me, I would prefer a different testimony. (I suppose we would all like to rewrite some portion of our lives.) But time and time again, I've seen that God uses what I have been through and what I've learned to "recycle." Yes, learned!

God can even "recycle" what we've learned—even from our very mundane experiences (like being chased by goats or running over chickens).

Even motorcycles?

Yes, even motorcycles.

Fourteen

Dusting and Praying

Be joyful always; pray continually; give thanks in all circumstances,
for this is God's will for you in Christ Jesus.
1 Thessalonians 5:16–18

Occasionally, when I am waiting for David to meet me at the Nashville Airport, I find myself looking for, you guessed it, country music stars. (Once a tourist, always a tourist!) And sometimes I spot people I know my kids would love to meet. Once I got an autograph from Steven Curtis Chapman and scored big points with Chera Kay. Another day I got the lead singer for the Newsboys to sign a little note for Zachary. (It really helps when I add these items to the free soaps and bags of peanuts.) And I'll never forget the time I spotted Vestal Goodman in the baggage claim area.

Normally, I would have grabbed a pad and pencil and gotten an autograph for my mom, because she is one of my mother's all-time favorite gospel music singers. But on this particular day I knew I needed a little bit more than an autograph. So I pushed through the crowd at baggage claim to get closer to Vestal.

You see, I'd had the opportunity to meet Vestal on several occasions during the taping of some of the Bill Gaither Homecoming videos. Being on the same platform—in the same studio—with Vestal Goodman as she sang and testified convinced me that she has a clear and direct line to the throne room of God. The woman can pray; and when she prays, you know it. So when I spotted her with her husband, Howard, and her pastor, the Reverend Johnny Menick, I had one of the best ideas I've ever had.

Mother had been especially ill that week because her white count had dropped so dangerously low from rounds and rounds of chemotherapy.

I stepped up close to Vestal and said, "Sister Vestal, do you remember me?"

Her face brightened, and she said, "Why, sure I do, honey!"

We talked for a bit about the latest videotaping and made small talk. Where are you flying home from? Staying busy? When was the last time you saw so-and-so? You know, airport chitchat.

Then before we said good-bye, I asked her what I had intended to ask all along, "Sister Vestal would you please pray for my mother? She is going through some tough chemotherapy treatments right now. Just sometime during your devotions this week please remember her."

That afternoon I learned that Vestal Goodman doesn't wait until her devotions to pray for someone. As a matter of fact, she doesn't wait for anything when it comes to prayer. In one swift motion she pulled her trademark handkerchief from her purse, laid a hand upon my shoulder and started praying, out loud—real loud.

The verse came to mind, "Where two or three are gathered together in my name, there am I in the midst of them" (Matthew 18:20, KJV). She waved her hanky and rebuked this "demon called cancer" to flee from my mother, in the name of Jesus. She shouted out (yes, shouted) "our thanks for the mercies of God and our gratefulness for his grace to make it through our troubled hour." She praised "the most powerful name ever spoken" and beamed as his glory shone across her face. Didn't I tell you? The woman can pray. And pray, we did!

Mom lived only a couple of miles from my house, so on our way home we stopped to see how she was holding up. When I had left her a couple of days before, she was just starting a fresh dose of chemotherapy, and that always took its toll. On these days when she would feel so bad, she would usually wear her housecoat with a cap to cover her head and sit in her soft chair and watch Gaither videos all day.

David and I pulled into the driveway. The few flowers in the beds by the front sidewalk were a reminder that Mother was not well—usually the beds were full and overflowing with pansies and geraniums. Before I had a chance to place my finger on the doorbell, the front door flew open. Mother was standing there—dressed in the bright, flowered print clothes she likes to wear—with the brightest grin across her face. She wouldn't let me get a word in. She just stepped out onto the porch and said, "Let me show you something very precious, honey."

We walked to the far corner of her porch, and she pointed to a bird's nest made of sticks and mud balanced right in the middle of the porch railing. She had been watching for weeks as this robin built its nest, filled it with eggs, and then finally hatched her young. What a wonder-filled way for her to pass the time when she had become confined to her house. She gestured for me to keep quiet and to walk slowly. Little by little I moved close enough until I was able to see the tiny pieces of light blue egg shells that lay around the edges of the nest, and three brand-new baby robins—hardly dry—stretched their necks and raised their heads upward, mouths open.

Still hushed, we tiptoed backwards. When we were far enough back, she said, "Honey, you're not going to believe this, but I feel better than I have in a long time. A little bit ago I was sitting in my chair when all of a sudden I felt this burst of energy just flow through me. And I just know it was the Lord."

Mother has witnessed the Lord's handiwork over the years, and I trusted she was correct this time.

"And," continued Mother, "I think the Lord is using these baby birds to teach me that there is still life left for me. I just know he is healing my body."

"Mother," I began, still almost in a whisper, "you'll never guess what happened at the airport . . . ."

My mother amazes me. Her faith is so firm that she didn't seem surprised at all at what God was doing. (Though she was a little surprised that I hadn't asked for Vestal's autograph.)

A Place for God

As far back as I can remember God has been around. When I say around, I mean my mother has always talked to God and about

God as if he were sitting on the other end of her sofa. I can remember Mom praying at the kitchen sink and at our bedsides. Dad would pray in the car before we left for school and again later at the supper table. God was in our house so much that I often wondered why we didn't just set an extra place at the table for him. But it would be years later before I would really understand the enormous power of prayer.

There are two mind-boggling things about our God that are beyond my comprehension (well, actually more than two but for now...): (1) He's got his hand on the timing of the whole world, and (2) his work of grace in our lives seems to be in some amazing way tied to the prayers of his people.

Martin Luther said, "Prayer is a powerful thing, for God has bound and tied himself thereto. None can believe how powerful prayer is, and what it is able to effect, but those who have learned it by experience."

I want to share with you a very personal and true story about my encounter with the supernatural power of prayer.

Prayer Power

Very early in my ministry work I was struggling to "find my place." (Have there ever been times when you just wanted God to give you the whole picture before you would really commit to signing up for the job? Or am I the only one who has ever struggled with that!?) I knew God was "sending me out," but I was hoping for a nine-to-five job. I seemed to be going through an emotional tug of war between what I thought I wanted and what I sensed God wanted. I think on some basic level Satan was holding me captive—in bondage to "self." I wasn't able to "let go and let God" direct me. (Mom said I needed one of those sermons she grew up with, one where the preacher would preach a good old-fashioned message on "dying out to self"! But that sounded painful to me.)

One weekend I was scheduled to speak at a women's event just north of Fort Wayne, Indiana. The kind women who picked me up at the airport drove me to a small cottage near the tabernacle of this beautiful Pentecostal campground. They teased me about placing me in that particular cabin called "Nazareth." (They'd heard I had grown up Nazarene.)

I had arrived early and had hours to spare. So after I unpacked my suitcase, I decided to take a quick nap. I dozed off listening to the silence, broken only by the sound of birds chirping in the early afternoon.

I don't know how long I had been sleeping, but I woke up terrified. The room was dark—hazy. There was an acrid odor that caused me to jump up and rush to the kitchen to check all the knobs on the stove, thinking the gas had been left on—but the appliances were all electric. Someone was in the cottage with me. Who and how? And why were they being so secret? Is that what I was smelling?

"Hello?" I called out. Just silence, dead silence. Not someone, but *something* was in the room. I could sense as much. I was trembling. There was something terribly wrong going on here. I didn't want to admit it right away (mainly because I had never experienced anything quite like this before), but what I was experiencing was far more than just fear—what I was sensing could only be described as *evil*.

I glanced across the tiny living room of this cottage and noticed my Bible lying on the couch. I made my way to the Bible and dropped to my knees by the couch, and I began to cry. There was no time to analyze, no time to "get a hold of myself," there was no thought of just "shrugging this off." Mother had always said there was power in the Word, so I began to quote every verse I had ever memorized as a child, from "Jesus wept" to "Greet one another with a holy kiss." And I began to plead the blood of Jesus; I began to pour out my heart and my fears to God and to ask for his protection.

I told Satan that I was a daughter of the King of kings and he had no place in my life, that there was no bondage or strongholds for him to keep me from serving the God I love and the God who I know loves me. Still on my knees I buried my face into the couch cushions. The longer I prayed the bolder I got! The more I called on the Holy Spirit, the less fear held my heart captive. This lasted only a few moments. And when I sensed the darkness had passed, I was both exhausted and exhilarated.

I lifted my head and a beautiful fragrance, as aromatic as fresh gardenias, filled the room. A ray of sunshine was beaming into the picture window and made a bright patch across the carpet. I could only stare at the brilliant light and grin. And I laughed. (I know if anyone had walked in at that moment, she would have committed me!) But like the light through the window, peace flooded my soul, and the "presence" I had felt earlier had vanished—and was replaced by another that seemed to recline comfortably at the end of the sofa.

I "died to self" that day. (I think an old-fashioned sermon would have been easier.) As far as I was concerned, I wanted to serve a God who could drive away the putridness of self and Satan. The One who could calm such fears that the evil one had tried to manipulate.

I learned that day what I had always been taught: We are privileged to tap into a power source far greater than any fear that Satan sends our way. And we do that with prayer. Oswald Chambers states it simply: "The very powers of darkness are paralyzed by prayer." Paralyzed. That day in Fort Wayne, I was trembling, but within moments the evil one was paralyzed, and I was smelling gardenias.

Denise's Story

Let me tell you another story, of how my friend Denise learned about the power of prayer. The first time I ever worked with Denise, we hit it off as good friends.

My first impression of Denise was that she was happy—I mean really happy. She had a great job and a great apartment. She talked about the sunsets at her favorite beach, the latest comic strip that made her cackle out loud, her flair for decorating and her goal to be "Martha Stewart" someday. (Okay, Denise introduced me to the name of Martha Stewart.) Denise knew the latest news about everything and everybody, from the new fall styles in Paris to the latest architectural trends in San Antonio. She could tell you the scoop from DC to LA and all the best restaurants in-between. She was just simply all together. (Another phrase she introduced me to!)

Late one night, after a lengthy television taping, Denise and I decided to grab a midnight bite at the Waffle House. (I know, I know. But all the health food restaurants that I love so much were already closed!) We ate our omelets, laughed about the funny things that had happened earlier that evening, and then headed back to the car.

Suddenly Denise grew serious. "Chonda, I'm going to tell you something. I think maybe it will explain why we are drawn together." We slipped into the front seat of her car and she spoke very softly, as if each word were painful for her to express. She told me the story of one horrible night when she was about twenty years old.

"I was up late watching a movie. I was living in Utah. My folks lived in Dallas. About 2 A.M. I heard a noise in my apartment. At first I thought it was one of my roommates getting up for some water. Then I heard the sound of things breaking. So I went to investigate and saw two men in dark clothes and ski masks. They had my roommate face down on the floor with a gun pointed at her, threatening to 'blow her head off.' Before I could scream or run, they grabbed me and began to roll black electrical tape around my wrists. Then they wrapped the tape around my head, over my eyes, again and again. They stripped off my clothes, dragged me into the bedroom and—raped me. They then threw a blanket around me, carried me out of the apartment and put me in the back of their car."

Denise was staring at the dashboard as she spoke, avoiding eye contact with me, working hard to relate a sequence of events that was not over yet.

"Because of the tape, I couldn't move my jaw to call out for help. I could see through a small gap in the tape, but to do that was painful because the adhesive would stick to my eyelashes and then my eyes would water. So I'd see for a quick moment: beer cans; then close my eyes. Then I'd open them again: a bag with a pair of sneakers sticking out. Then I'd rest them again. I tried to remember everything—the turns the car made, every smell."

She paused and I was about to reach for her, to hug her, when she just sighed and continued on.

"They took me out to the edge of town and pulled me out of the car. They made me stand with my face against a cold, hard wall with the blanket barely across my back. I thought they were going to shoot me execution style. I finally began to cry but could barely make a sound. The tears moistened the tape around my eyes and I could see more through the tiny slit: it was a brick wall. Suddenly, I heard car doors slam and the sound of a car speeding away. As I turned away from the wall, I could hear the snow crunch under my sock feet, but I couldn't feel anything because the cold had numbed my soles. I collapsed against the wall and followed it to the ground. I worked my hands loose and then got the tape off my eyes. I couldn't believe it. I knew where I was. They had taken me to a school about two blocks from a police station."

I sat motionless in the front seat of her car. She wiped at her eyes with a napkin she had brought from the Waffle House. Although this had happened more than fifteen years before, it was obviously still very painful for her to talk about. All I knew to do was to lean across the car seat and throw my arms around her and cry. (I had to borrow her napkin, but she was finished with it.) She just patted me on the back as if to say, "I'm okay. Really I am."

"So you see, Chonda," she eventually said, "we do have some things in common."

I shook my head. "No, Denise," I said emphatically. "I can't imagine your pain or your fear and anger."

It seems that's not what she meant. She continued. "We may not have common pain—but we have a common healer."

I wanted her to keep talking, to answer my questions: How do you sleep at night? How do you keep from being scared to death at every noise in your house? How do you laugh at a late night movie, or sit and enjoy a funny book? How do you keep finding joy in your life?

Christian counselors, new friends, a different city, and an exciting church were all tools that Denise believes the Lord used to help her get through her trauma to a place of healing. But no tool, she feels, was more instrumental than the prayer of another.

She took a deep breath and continued to tell me the rest of the story. Hundreds of miles away, on that same night, a woman named Diane was awakened by the Lord and told to pray. She had never met Denise. But Diane had been compelled to get out of her bed and to pray for hours for someone—a stranger—whom she felt was hurting and in need of help.

Diane continued to pray for this unknown person for several days. And then, later that week, she attended a chapel service at the company where she worked. She listened intently as a coworker stood and vulnerably laid out his anger and sorrow for the pain his daughter had recently suffered. He was Denise's father. As he told Denise's story, related the hour and the day, Diane began to weep. She knew she'd been praying for Denise. She recognized what God was doing—calling on a sister to intercede for another who was in great peril.

It would be ten years before Diane and Denise would actually meet face-to-face. And Denise beamed when she told me about the opportunity to thank her long-distance rescuer for being obedient to God's call to pray.

Praying While You Work

I'm so grateful that my mother taught her children to pray. By the time we were putting sentences together on our own, Mother would encourage us to talk to God in our own words. Believe me, "God is great, God is good, Let us thank him for our food" just didn't cut it at our house. As we grew older "Good bread, good meat, dear Lord, let's eat!" didn't cut it either. (It prompted a swift kick under the table—but that's another story!) I remember running it in at mealtime; every one of us kids would race to slap a fist down on the table with the thumb up. The last to do so had to pray. (We'd learned this at youth camp.) If Mother saw this, she'd slap our hands away and make whoever started it pray.

Mother also taught me that talking to God was not simply giving him my wish list. She would quip, "God doesn't wear a red suit and jump down the chimney."

In her book *Miracles Happen When You Pray*, Quin Sherrer says, "It is important to recognize that prayer is not a way to manipulate God." Rather than trying to manipulate God to get what you want, why not spend some intimate moments getting to know what *God* wants?

Believe me, we've all had our prayers answered in ways we didn't particularly like. I could name a few: David didn't get the raise we needed. No one came by to help me change the tire in the rain (not even David). And Cheralyn wasn't healed; she died. But as the years go by, I have learned that "getting what we want" is not nearly as rewarding as the personal relationship available to us with the One who is listening to our requests.

And true intimacy with your heavenly Father begins with moments of adoration and exhortation. He already knows what is going on in your troubled soul. So reach out and embrace his love for you by speaking words of love to him. And when the pain is so heavy that there are no words to speak, that's okay too. He hears our moans and groans—our utterances—and he always has an answer. "In the same way, the Spirit helps us in our weakness. We do not know what we ought to pray for, but the Spirit himself intercedes for us with groans that words cannot express" (Romans 8:26).

Prayer can heal, as I believe it did with my mother. Prayer can protect you from evil, as I sensed it did for me that day in Fort Wayne. Prayer can come from loved ones or even strangers and can protect you from grave danger, as it did for my friend Denise. What a powerful tool God has equipped us with.

One of the biggest excuses I hear about prayer is "I just don't have the time to pray." Frankly, that's an excuse for not cleaning the house—not for not praying. I hate cleaning the house. (Just look under the furniture!) But even that dreaded chore offers an opportunity to pray—and often those prayers are for my children. When Quin Sherrer was a young woman, Catherine Marshall urged her to "Be as specific in your prayers as you can, and plant waiting prayers for your children's future."

Every time I clean Zachary's room, I pray for him—specifically for his future (sometimes that the lid on the jar that houses some scaly-looking creature is on tight) and for his safety. While picking Chera's clothes up off the floor, I pray for her—for God's continued anointing on her life, about her eagerness to grow up, for his will in her life. In the kitchen, I pray for my family. In our room, I pray for my marriage, for my husband as he faces the challenges of leading this household. I may miss a few spots while dusting furniture, but I am busy and thorough planting prayers for our future and the future of my children.

Praying while you work is no substitute to the commitment to meet with God intimately. But it is a good way to get you started in tapping into the greatest thing you can ever do for your family.

A parent, a child, a friend, yourself. You are surrounded by cause to pray, and to pray diligently—without ceasing. And if you can anticipate that there will be dark days ahead—as experience has so often proved—then why not pray today for sunshine for tomorrow? To come sooner, without delay, to shine with a brilliance so that the darkness will be dispersed. Planting and sunshine go together. Just like housecleaning and praying.

Fifteen

Preparation: The Key to Survival

Your word is a lamp to my feet and a light for my path.
Psalm 119:105

You can never be too prepared, Mom," my fourteen-year-old daughter, Chera Kay, admonished as we loaded the van for a week-long camping trip. Correction: a five-day, three-hour, forty-minute, and thirteen-second camping trip! (But who's counting?)

It was a hot July morning, and David, following his manly urges, had made the decision a few weeks earlier to teach his children everything he knew about surviving in the wilderness of the Great Smoky Mountains National Park (which was why I insisted on the campsite nearest the ranger's station).

We had planned this trip for some time. Chera Kay loves the outdoors. For weeks she had been watching the Discovery Channel and surfing the Internet for information about poisonous plant roots, berries, and leaves. She retains more knowledge than my bread machine. She once told me that the average person swallows ten microscopic spiders every year. (No way. Not at the Holiday Inn, they don't!)

Our eight-year-old son, Zachary, on the other hand, thinks that "roughing it" is going a night with a broken VCR and no Pop Tarts. "This trip's going to be real good for Zachary," I told David as we packed the van with the essentials—bug spray, charcoal lighter, lots of plastic stuff from Wal-Mart, toilet paper, more bug spray. Zach needed to get away from the TV, the Nintendo, and his Little League baseball team—the Killers.

We had no trouble finding the wilderness. But on the four-hour drive east into Daniel Boone country, the batteries ran down on Zachary's Game Boy.

"Hey, Zachary, this is going to be the greatest week of your life!" I said, trying to cheer him up.

"Right. When do we get to the Ramada Inn?"

Admittedly, it was difficult not to side up with Zachary and, as the official navigator, point David and the van into the nearest hotel parking lot. As a matter of fact, I have a signed "camping contract" with my family: After five days we find a hotel with room service, a hot shower, and a remote control. David and Chera Kay will just have to use their imaginations: Two of those big fluffy Marriott pillows and a table lamp make a great pup tent!

I had envisioned a quaint campfire where giant logs had been cut and stacked to make stools and the musical ringing of invisible crickets could soothe away the knots brought on by a stressful day. But first it rained. We sat in the van on a muddy road and waited for it to stop.

After the dark clouds blew over, David and Chera worked to "set up camp." They wrestled the tent from off the top of the van to the wet ground, while Zach and I unpacked the picnic supplies and set them on the wet picnic table.

David had brought along some new stuff guaranteed to start a fire faster—and every time. He scraped and sparked for a long time, just like the instructions said. Finally, he wadded up the instructions and lit the fire with a big wooden match he'd found in the bottom of the glove box.

Chera stacked up muddy, wet timber on the pyramid-shaped pile that was producing more smoke than fire. "Smoke follows beauty," David shouted when the black plume whipped through camp and nearly choked me to death.

"Can we go to McDonald's?" Zach asked.

I made a mental note to renegotiate my camping contract.

Our first meal was an open-flame delicacy: blackened hot dogs. And that first evening we breathed in the fresh smells of God's open country: burning wood, bug spray, and burnt plastic (we had set the cooler too close to the fire). As the night grew late, we decided to turn in.

So here we were, at 7:30 P.M., sitting in the four-man tent, our humble home for the next, count them, **five** days. David and Chera huddled over a hiking map, routing the best trail for our morning venture to Laurel Falls. Chera Kay would be our camp guide. Her backpack was loaded with everything we might need: a compass, waterproof matches, a piece of flint (in case the matches really did get wet!), a first-aid kit, Gummy Bears, and a book to help her identify edible mushrooms, roots, and bugs.

Chera tried to convince Zachary that hiking would be much more fun than Nintendo. "Come on, Zach. This is going to be fun. We'll pick up the trailhead at Cosby and hike back about 200 meters until we reach approximately 2,200 feet altitude. There I'm sure we'll find some wonderful specimens of mountain laurel, perhaps some May apple plants and—if we're real lucky—the Tennessee cockleshell plant." Her grin was as wide as the tent flap.

Zachary punched in vain at the on/off switch on the Game Boy, sighed, and said, "Stop telling me stuff, Chera."

"I just don't want any of us getting lost out there," Chera said, waving a hand into the wide-open darkness.

"Chera, I can find the trails by myself. . . . Besides, boys can hike better than girls."

Uh-oh. Sometimes Zachary has to learn things the hard way.

"Okay, guys," I said, recognizing the appropriate time to interrupt. "I've got a good way to pass the time."

"How?" David, Chera, and Zach asked in harmony.

"Sleep."

With enough sleep, I figured our five days would pass by faster, and before long I'd be soaking in a tub at the nearest Best Western!

I snuggled close to Zach and said, "Let's try to name all the sounds we hear tonight. Listen. I hear a few crickets."

After a long pause Chera whispered, "There's a frog croaking out there somewhere, Zach. Do you hear it?"

David, who, by the way, teaches English at a local university, noticed the "muffled rasping sound of the trees brushing against the night sky as the tines of a rake would furrow the fertile soil." (Professors! Go figure!)

Zachary wasn't going to sleep. Suddenly—at last—he was capturing the spirit of nature. *Begone the terrors of the city and the harshness of civilization!* He cupped a hand to his ear and whispered, "And, Mom, I bet if we get real quiet, we can hear the screams of people getting eaten by bears!"

We were all silenced. We were actually listening. I was afraid to even breathe. Then Zach giggled, and we all began to laugh. After a while we talked about our upcoming hike to Laurel Falls.

"We'll need hiking sticks."

"Is there a trail on the map that is downhill going there *and* coming back?"

"Does poison ivy have three leaves or five?"

"Does this bug spray keep away snakes, or is there a different spray for that?"

"Take plenty of candy bars in case we get lost."

One by one we fell asleep—and no one got eaten by bears.

Did you know that there are birds in the Smoky Mountains that chirp louder than my alarm clock? They start at about 4:45 A.M. and go on and on. Forget about snooze control. When I got up to start breakfast sometime shortly after sunrise, David was already working on the fire. (I got the feeling he wasn't very happy with his guaranteed fire-starting stuff.) When he saw me up and ready to work, he left the pretty stack of wood and lit the portable gas stove.

Chera rolled out of the tent just as the bacon began sizzling. She was already dressed, complete with her new hiking boots and green hiking socks. Her backpack, full of essentials, was draped across one shoulder. "Well, Mom," she said, just as chipper as any bird in the mountains, "are you ready to take the mountain?"

"Oh sure, Chera. Believe me, I was hiking Mount Everest before you were ever born...."

"Oh right," Chera said, "and here comes the other hiking expert in this family."

We looked at the tent and saw Zachary emerge, his hair sticking straight up at odd angles, as if he'd been wrestling bears all night. He was rubbing his eyes and scratching his bare stomach. (He is so much like his father!) Without saying a word to anyone, he walked around the tent maybe four times, like something straight out of the Old Testament. About the fifth time around he shouted with great exasperation and urgency, "Will somebody tell me— where's the doggone trail to the bathroom?!"

Cleaning Up

I'd like to say that everything was fun after that and we all laughed like the Brady Bunch in their little squares at the beginning of their show. But camping out was a week of muddy mess, smoke in our eyes, and teeny tiny gravel that lay underneath my sleeping bag every night. As a matter of fact, I don't think there was a whole lot of laughing going on until we were safely checked in at the Budgetel Inn and we remembered how funny Zach had looked racing around that tent.

That first night in the hotel room, Chera Kay began to unload her backpack. There was a snakebite kit we'd never used (Thank you, Lord!), her Swiss Army knife that came in handy when dividing up the last slice of pizza, a tiny magnifying glass we used to get the splinter out of Zach's finger (his Game Boy finger of all things!), and a big, pink, worn, and somewhat tattered, Bible. (Honest, *I* didn't put it there!)

As she unloaded everything, Chera proudly announced, "Well, I didn't get prepared for nothing!"

I am blessed to be my daughter's mother. Chera Kay is an outstanding young girl who never misses a single night of reading her Bible. And I know how lucky I am to have my daughter burst into my room occasionally (even at midnight) and yell, "Oh, Mother, listen to this verse. Isn't this the greatest?"

Chera takes her Bible with her wherever she goes. She takes it to school every day; she would never pack her backpack without it. Even when we're walking through the mall, Chera carries her "sword," as she calls it. (I'm not making any of this up. Is she a mother's dream, or what?)

Oswald Chambers says, "It is easy to imagine that we will get to a place where we are complete and ready, but preparation is not suddenly accomplished, it is a process steadily maintained. It is dangerous to get into a settled state of experience. It is preparation and preparation . . . and the 'go' of preparation is to let the word of God scrutinize."

The Greatest Survival Tool

I can remember, as a child, Sunday school teachers who rewarded me with candy bars for memorizing certain passages of Scripture. (I had crummy teeth, but I learned a lot of verses!) And my mother never stopped "training her children up in the way." Every day she would read the Bible to us, until we were old enough to read it ourselves. As I've taken this journey of mine, the Word has become the greatest survival tool in *my* "backpack."

But what good is an instruction manual if you never open it up? What good would a compass have been tucked away in the bottom of Chera's backpack if we had gotten lost in the "wilderness?"

My husband recently purchased a new thingamajig, which he calls a Global Positioning Satellite System. (When he wants to sound smart, he just calls it a GPS.) Anyway, this thingamabob links to a dozen different satellites in the sky. If we happen to be hiking in the woods (in a moment of insanity), then this whatchamacallit can guide us all safely home.

One afternoon, David wanted me to walk with him. (I believe he wanted to see how many ticks we could find in a day; we had lots of luck.) After a couple of hours (I was sure we had bagged our limit) and after crossing through the same slimy creek half-a-dozen times, I finally said, "Honey, are we lost?"

Silence.

Uh-oh.

At least there weren't any convenience stores around for us to pass again and again without stopping and asking for directions. I tried to cheer him up, so I said, "Why don't you take out that do-a-ma-hicky thing and find out where we are?"

Sheepishly he hung his head and mumbled, "It's in the trunk of the car. I forgot to bring it."

He could have had a hundred of those thingamajigs in the trunk (and he may have; I'll have to check on that), but if it's lost in the trunk somewhere, then we're lost in the wilderness somewhere else.

The apostle Paul writes, "Let the word of Christ dwell in you richly as you teach and admonish one another with all wisdom, and as you sing psalms, hymns and spiritual songs with gratitude in your hearts to God" (Colossians 3:16). Notice a difference here? It is not sufficient that we simply read the Word—it is imperative that the Word "dwell in you." You must do more than put it in your "backpack." You must take it out of the trunk and use it.

"The goal is not for us to get through the Scriptures," writes John Ortberg in his book *The Life You've Always Wanted*. "The goal is to get the Scriptures through us. Knowledge about the Bible is an indispensable good. But knowledge does not by itself lead to spiritual transformation." (By the way, I cannot recommend John Ortberg's book enough. Stick a bookmark in this spot right now, lay this book down, and then run, don't walk, to your local Christian bookstore, and ask for it!)

When I was growing up, it seemed like everyone in church was a Bible scholar. They knew (according to Scripture) how long my brother's hair should be, and they knew (according to Scripture) that we were supposed to love one another. And for years, I, too, memorized a lot of verses (and had the dental fillings to prove it), but until I allowed the Word of God to come alive, or as Paul puts it, to allow myself to be washed by the Word (see Ephesians 5:26), my compass (or GPS) was still in the trunk.

In life, as in comedy, there are moments when we wait, sometimes just hang on, watching and listening, wondering just where this journey is taking us. We're like Zach: The night has been long; we'd rather be anywhere else but here. Perhaps we're looking for the doggone trail to anywhere. Perhaps we packed all the right things, but we never use them. They stay in the trunk.

Well, you didn't get prepared for nothing. It's time to be washed by the Word. "Imagine having a mind cleansed of all debris that blocks our best intentions," John Ortberg writes. "Imagine if each time you saw another person your first thought was to pray for him or bless her. Imagine what it would be like if, any time you were challenged or anxious, your reflexive response would be to turn to God for strength . . . Imagine, genuinely wishing your 'enemies' well."

This is what it would be like to have our minds "washed by the Word," continues Ortberg. "This is what it would be like to 'let the word of Christ dwell in you richly.' This is how we are to be transformed by Scripture. This is our great need."

You may be more prepared than you ever realized. Maybe your compass is in the bottom of your backpack. Maybe your knowledge needs to pour out from your head and wash down into your heart. Maybe it's time for a good washing!

When we returned from the mountains, we had a mountain of laundry. "Family laundry time!" I called. So we spent the next few hours sorting (David didn't understand this process at all), then I sent David to the store for some detergent. (He took his GPS.) We poured in a cup of detergent (guaranteed to smell like the great outdoors), and everything was ready to go.

David looked at the washer, he looked at me, he looked at his GPS. "Now what do we do?" he asked.

I sighed, pushed a little button, and said, "We add water."

John Ortberg puts it this way: "When a mind is washed—when someone begins to be filled with the very thoughts of God—it is a gift to the world."

Are you ready for anything? It's not enough to just *know* the words, you understand. You have to allow the words to wash over you. Before you spend some time reading God's Word today, ask him to wash you with the words so they might dwell in you—transform you. (Or as my husband would now say, "Take the GPS out of the trunk, and use it!") Then you'll be prepared for anything.

Sixteen

Lost and Found in Cincinnati

I thank my God every time I remember you. In all my prayers for all of you,
I always pray with joy because of your partnership in the gospel from the first
day until now, being confident of this, that he who began a good work in you
will carry it on to completion until the day of Christ Jesus.

(Philippians 1:3–6)

I had been in Cincinnati many times before, but never in the Riverfront Coliseum, or with the Women of Faith Conference, or before 16,000 women and in the company of such incredible speakers as Luci Swindoll, Marilyn Meberg, Barbara Johnson, Thelma Wells, and, of course, Patsy Clairmont. I was pretty intimidated to say the least. I walked (barely) into the hospitality room (greenroom) and waited for my appointed hour. I was nervous. All these incredible women speakers, authors, professionals—and me!

The atmosphere was as heavy as the reference section of a library, but things began to lighten up after they rolled a small TV set into the room. Then we could see what was happening on the main stage of the coliseum. As quickly as the TV warmed up, the greenroom felt less like a greenroom and more like a locker room at a football game! Those women rolled up their sleeves and began to cheer one another on. They weren't competitors, but comrades, teammates. In time an usher would poke her head in the door and say something like, "Okay, Patsy. You're up." Then Barbara... Everyone else would pat the woman of the hour on the back and start yelling things like, "Go get 'em girl! You the woman! Knock 'em dead!"

I thought that at any minute someone would whip out a chalkboard and draw a few *O*'s and *X*'s in the middle. Luci would shout,

"Okay, Marilyn, I'm going to hand the ball off over here. Barbara, you run down the middle and fake the pass. Patsy will slip around and block the tackle . . . ." I wanted to shout, "What about me? What do you want me to do?" But I couldn't muster a squeak in this room. I did discover why they call it the *greenroom*. I think it's for the rookies, like me, because of the particular shade of green that covered my face!

Everyone else seemed to have loosened up, but the tension never diminished for me. I couldn't pull my gaze away from the door. I knew my turn was coming soon. Then it happened; the usher leaned into the room: "Uh, Condra Price?" (Like I said, I was the obvious rookie!) "It's your turn."

The usher led me down a dark corridor and through some giant curtains. (The thought occurred to me that perhaps I should drop some bread crumbs in case I had to find my way back.) As we turned the corner, I could hear the distinct roaring sound of applause. I could see the bright lights, stage lights. But suddenly the lights dimmed. Someone slipped off the platform and the MC took her place. I don't remember a word of her introduction. I just remember looking up and around and behind and to the left and to the right—there were women everywhere. I couldn't help it. I did what I always do when I get nervous: I started laughing. Some of it came because of my nerves. The other reason was because I couldn't wait to see how in the world God was going to get me out of this one!

You see, I've never considered myself a fancy conference speaker or a real singer. I'm just a comedian. (And to tell you the truth, I don't know when someone tagged that title to my name.) I tell stories—some are funny, some are not. And here I was, telling my story to more than 16,000 women.

Doris, who plays the piano for me and travels with me nearly everywhere I go, was with me on this day. We had driven up from Nashville the night before, and together, the next morning, we set up the booth with some videotapes, cassettes, and books. We learned that not just any old building is called a coliseum—just gigantic ones! And this place was. On top of that, it was round. We thought we could get the job done in no time—grab a snack and a shower and be ready for the evening event. We borrowed a cart to carry some boxes from the van to the booth—a simple short trip, but we kept getting lost.

"Does any of this look familiar?" I asked Doris politely enough.

"I recognize that pretzel stand." We were getting hungry.

When we passed the same pretzel guy for the third time, we got so tickled we had to stop. "How do we keep missing our table?!" I said. We took a moment to catch our breath. We stopped by a window where I could see across the Cincinnati skyline. A sudden realization made me laugh. "I'm right back where I started," I said.

Doris laughed too and said, "I know. Let's just keep walking. I think your table is just around the bend."

"No, really, I'm right back where I started. Literally right back where I began."

From where I was standing I could see across the Ohio River. The skyline looked like a losing round of Tetris (my favorite video game) with an additional pointed church steeple here and there. I pointed in the direction of the bridge that led into Covington, Kentucky, and said, "Look, Doris. Over there somewhere is an old boarded-up building that used to be Saint Elizabeth Hospital. That's where I was born."

All the years that had gone by. All the events. All this time had passed. The laughs. The stories. And here I was, within minutes of where I had started, literally! Not only was this my birthplace, but the last I had heard, somewhere near the Cincinnati area lived a man I hadn't seen or heard from in over seven years: my father. Most of his family lived in this area as well. This conference had been comprehensively advertised. Surely someone would want to see how I was, see me all grown up, maybe want to see pictures of my kids. In over twenty years since my parents' divorce, I had heard from his family only once or twice. But I had thought about them a lot.

So here I stood, years later, wondering if he knew I was here, wondering if anyone would show up to see me, waiting for a kind word, wondering what I'd do if they did come. I recalled those feelings as a teenage girl, standing on the front porch of our home, wondering if he'd ever come home, waiting for a birthday card from my grandmother, a note from an aunt—uncertain about the future, anxiously waiting for some affirmation.

"What incredible timing, Lord," I thought. "Am I really ready for a conference like this? Here? Has my entire life led up to this? Have I actually come full circle? Is this what it's all been for? Is this the fullness of my time?" Maybe so. But for right now, we had some boxes to move.

God's Clock Keeps Perfect Time

The MC announced my name and someone else handed me a microphone, and somehow I opened my mouth. I'm not sure how I got through the night with so much on my mind. How did I tell my story, deliver the punch lines, pause in the right places? How was my timing? I'm not sure. But God's timing was impeccable, as always. His love runs deeper than the circumstances, rejections, hurts, or pains. His Holy Spirit always shows up when we invite him into every moment in our lives. Always right on time at just the right moment.

And it was a moment, to say the least. We had a blast! They laughed and I laughed. They cried and I cried. You have to believe me when I say this, but the applause isn't why I do my job. (I've worked a few times and heard very little applause when I was done. Ugh!)

But that evening, in less than forty-five minutes, I had received three standing ovations—and I will tell you, honestly, it felt good! It was a sweet sound of affirmation for the part of me who still felt like a teenager waiting on the front porch—alone and insecure.

When I left town the next morning, the applause was still ringing in my ears, and yet . . . I left with a bit of disappointment. No long-lost relative had left a message at the hall—or at the hotel—asking to see me, wishing me well, saying I'd done a great job.

Some weeks later I got a letter in the mail. I noticed the postmark almost immediately: Covington, Kentucky. Maybe this is the note I'd been looking for earlier?

I opened it and began to read a long letter from a stranger named Teresa. She is about my age, a preacher's daughter who lives within a few blocks of my birthplace.

Her mother had given her a ticket to the Women of Faith Conference as a Christmas gift. She wrote, "If it hadn't been a gift, I would have never gone." She went on to explain that she didn't have a real strong relationship with her parents.

"My life was pretty much in shambles before the Joyful Journey weekend. It has been almost twelve years since I have darkened the door of any church or sat and listened to any Christian speaker. I think God had sent a few hints to me that He was still with me, but I chose to ignore them.

"The odd thing is, Chonda, if I had heard you ten years ago—or maybe even ten days earlier—you might have made me laugh, but I'm not sure I was ready to reveal the real side of me. The need. The pain. The honesty. The time just wouldn't have been right."

She wrote about her relationship with her husband and children, about how she knew that she was within weeks of walking out on both. She had been so hopeless—to the point of suicide. She continued.

"I went to the conference simply to keep from arguing with my mother and sat in the middle of those 16,000 women. But that day, you were there to talk directly to me.

"You popped out onstage out of nowhere! And God knew the time was right. I was caught up in the laughter. And then, when you had all my attention, you ripped my heart out. As tears rolled down my face, I had flashbacks of my own pain in the past and how I had let it paralyze me. All this time, I had not looked for God. I had shut him out. I had wasted all this time. You made me see that I am not alone. You told me the truth, and it set me free. And the truth is, even God's children may suffer, but the whole time he is always there. I will never forget the peace I experienced that day once I realized that.

"You poured out your life so that I could find joy and peace. I made the decision that day that no matter what, I would raise my children in church. I went to church for the first time in twelve years the following Sunday. And today, I am excited about my new life in Christ, and I just wanted to write you and thank you."

Tears were flowing down my cheeks and spilled onto her pages. (Sometimes I am a messy reader.) I had caught God at it again. His timing was at work. Teresa sensed that if she'd heard my story just months before, she would not have been ready to respond. It was a good reminder to me that restoration cannot be forced—not even by a comedian. And yet God is at work—in his time. And, as Corrie ten Boom said, "God's clock keeps perfect time!"

From beginning to end, God has been at work in the lives of his people. Oh, there may be times when you quit looking for him. Perhaps you stopped allowing him to work; you stopped acknowledging his Lordship. Perhaps you think his time clock is moving too slow, that his timing is holding you back. But let me tell you, life in Jesus is the most liberating life of all. Leaning on him allows you to stand. Holding onto his Word doesn't tie you down; it gives you the freedom to soar in peace and contentment, knowing he is in control, trusting that in his time, he will work all things for good—that life with him brings happiness.

Hallmark Days

Since the Women of Faith weekend, I have made a few trips to Northern Kentucky to visit with Teresa. We have become friends, woven together by one moment in time when God allowed our paths to cross. I stopped by for a visit with her just weeks ago, while working on this book. I think I was having one of those melancholy moments. I call them my Hallmark Days—when everything I write or think about sounds like a Hallmark Card commercial! We talked for a long time, and when I heard her laugh, I saved it for my collection, knowing here is one I can hold up to the sun and marvel at, one that has been through the fire—her life is more evidence that though life may be dark, the fun will indeed come up.

On this particular visit I pulled off the interstate while on my way home. I guess curiosity got the best of me once again, and I decided to look for my grandmother's old house. She passed away several years ago, but I still have aunts and uncles on my father's side living in the area. I think I was fourteen or fifteen years old the last time I was at her house. So why look now? Honestly? Maybe it's the same emotion that still causes me to seek other affirmation besides laughter and applause—once in a while I still battle that feeling of being somewhat "disconnected." Unwanted. Forgotten. I just wanted to see that house from the outside.

So I drove down streets I vaguely remembered—some back and forth so much that I didn't know if I remembered them from twenty years ago or just ten minutes before—when I was lost. I had hoped to find the old house and maybe pause there for a moment, find buttercups she had planted when I was a little girl, reflect on how large the house and yard had seemed then, and maybe even find an old bracelet I had lost there as a child and remember . . . (see how my mind can wander when I'm lost?).

Well, I never found her house. I'm not as good with directions as I thought I was. You know what I did find? A sweet affirmation from God—better than any applause—in knowing that no matter how far I go, how desperately I search to fill empty voids in my life, no matter how low I stoop or how high I climb, he is always there. Always.

I never take a road trip without a Bryan Duncan tape. Even Mother loves his music. It's just been tough convincing her that his first solo album, "Anonymous Confessions of a Lunatic Friend," really is a Christian album! As I made my way back toward the interstate I listened to one of Bryan's tapes, and the Holy Spirit used these words to comfort me as Bryan sang:

And we all feel lost sometimes,
And we all feel hurt inside
And we all cry,
And we all need
The redeeming love of Jesus.

Sometimes "we all feel lost," we all feel pain and need to cry. And on those days, every one of us needs "the redeeming love of Jesus."

In the car that day I was reminded of the broadness of God's love—one Savior—for so many. And yet God's knowledge of me and love for me is utterly personal—to meet the unique characteristics of my life and personality. He has personally customized his power, comfort, and grace to fit my specific need. One God, one love—yet he is uniquely my Father (and yours). How much more affirmation did I need than that? I searched no more and headed home—to my own front porch.

For years and years I had trouble understanding Romans 8:28: "And we know that in all things God works for the good of those who love him, who have been called according to his purpose." I could never see very much good in death. I could never see any good in divorce, in trials, in loneliness. My mother would always tell me that God was building character in me with the trials of my life. I'd spout off, "What's wrong with the character I am now?"

Trust-ercise

Twenty years later, I'm not sure I understand the *whys* much better. But I have become more sure of the God who knows *why*. And in placing my confidence in him, I've learned to laugh. As George MacDonald said, when we're sure of our God, we're not "afraid to laugh in his presence."

I have lived my life with Christ long enough now to have seen his hand at work so vividly that I don't struggle as often with trusting him. As a young girl in Sunday school I memorized the scripture verse: "Trust in the LORD with *all* your heart and lean not on your own understanding; in all your ways *acknowledge* him, and he will make your paths *straight*" (Proverbs 3:5, emphasis added).

Can I give you a simple exercise to do? A "trust-ercise"? Write that scripture verse down in big letters on a giant piece of paper. Now take a pair of scissors and cut each sentence out separately. Go ahead. I'll wait.

Now, arrange the sentences this way: (1) Lean not on your own understanding; (2) in all your ways acknowledge him; (3) trust in the Lord.

You see, learning to trust the Lord, even when we don't understand life's circumstances—that's a tough one. There are days that
I have to tape each sentence to my bathroom mirror and remind
myself that today—this day, I choose to "lean not on my own
understanding."

That's hard for me—especially back when I so much wanted
an answer to the big 'why?' Why did I have to face three devastat-
ing losses within the course of two years—when I was so very young
and vulnerable?

I think of what Warren Wiersbe wrote in *When Bad Things
Happen to God's People*: "When you and I hurt deeply, what we really
need is not an explanation from God but a revelation of God."

I've come to grips with times when "God doesn't make sense."
(I read James Dobson's book!) I know that God doesn't do horrible
things to people. But there have been times when I've felt a bit . . .
well, cheated, that such a big question as Why? is never answered.
Is asking why wrong? Not always. Elisabeth Elliot wrote, "There
are those who insist that it is a very bad thing to question God. To
them, "why?" is a rude question. That depends, I believe, on
whether it is an honest search, in faith, for his meaning, or whether
it is a challenge of unbelief and rebellion. The psalmist often ques-
tioned God and so did Job. God did not answer the questions, but
he answered the man—with the mystery of Himself" (Elisabeth
Elliot, *On Asking God Why*).

King Solomon wrote in Proverbs that we are not to lean on
our own understanding but to trust. Remember the trust-ercise:

1. Lean not on your own understanding.
2. In all your ways acknowledge him.
3. Trust in the Lord.

Wait a minute! We left out a sentence:

4. And he will make your paths straight.

Well, for me, I've learned that as I get the other three in line,
this one falls into place. (I don't have to tape this one to the mirror
as often.) You see, as I've trusted him with my past, as I've worried

less about the whys—I've learned I can trust him with my future. Worrying and wondering about the direction my path should take has diminished. As a matter of fact, there are a few days that I don't even think about the path at all. (Just a few!) After I admitted to him that "there are things I don't understand, but I acknowledge you, Lord; there are things I cannot fix, but I praise you, Father; there are things I just can't change, but you are my Lord; there are things that just aren't funny, but I know I love you, Lord," then, I found my indecision paled in comparison to his glory and joy.

Because when I'm sure of my God, I'm not afraid to laugh in his presence.

Every single one of us has a story to tell. (And you don't have to be a comedian!) Some may not always have a happy-ever-after ending, yet telling our stories and opening our hearts to one another can encourage others to follow him—and hopefully to trust him. If that happens to you, then it won't be too long before you'll stand on your own front porch and just laugh right out loud (in his presence!) regardless of how far you may have veered off the interstate. Because when you allow yourself to trust God, in spite of life's circumstances or disappointments, then "he will make your paths straight."

Seventeen

Mama Gets a New Do

A heart at peace gives life to the body.
Proverbs 14:30

For months I had stood helplessly on the sidelines as the strenuous cancer treatments, the chemotherapy, and the radiation took their toll on Mother: the nausea, the hair loss, the aches, the fear. In such a short time, it seemed Mother had experienced it all.

So when I told Mother that someone from The Nashville Network wanted to interview me and wanted her to be a part of it—she was doubly thrilled. (Mom's a ham—where do you think I get it!?) Because of Mom, everyone in the next three counties (and a few other states!) knew about our big day. Oh well, at least this would keep her mind occupied for a good forty-eight hours.

The new magazine show "American Skyline" was hosted by Lesley Hamer, and they were interested in showing a few personal highlights with me and the kids, candid shots of our interacting in our "natural habitat," and an interview with me for a few moments as I sat on the couch next to Mother and looked at old photo albums. I was excited only because I knew Mother needed the distraction. (Believe me, cleaning every corner of my house, convincing my kids to wear their Sunday best, and borrowing real china from my neighbor to make my "natural habitat" look impressive is not my idea of excitement!)

My mother has always been a fan of everything I do. I can't remember very many performances at Opryland when she wasn't sitting on the front row—beaming. (She missed one day when she passed out from heat exhaustion. But after a night's rest she was back the next day.) So there was no way that a dose of chemo would ever stop her from getting in on all the excitement! Besides, she only lived two blocks away. And one shouldn't complain about a mother who is proud of her daughter (unless she makes you try on underwear from some lady from the American Cancer Society!).

And speaking of humiliation! Early in the week of the interview, during one of our many trips to the radiologist, I noticed Mother's purse (satchel) seemed bulkier than usual—but I knew it was going to be a long day and she loved to pack a few snacks, so I didn't think much about it. Later, in the examining room, Mother unloaded some of her cargo: Chonda tapes, videos, and cassettes. "Oh, this is so nice," she told her doctor as she made neat, little stacks of product on the clean bed sheets, "because your daughter and my daughter have so much in common. They are both in Christian music. Isn't that just so nice, Dr. Grant?" My face went blood red. I was once again simultaneously glorified and mummified by my mother. (Did I mention that Mother's radiologist is Amy Grant's father?)

Just for kicks, on our way home from her radiation treatment that day, I drove Mom past Amy Grant's mansion-like house. I think she was a little disappointed that Amy and I didn't have more in common.

The taping was not going exactly as I had hoped or planned. I think my son is taking lessons from my mother on how to terrify me on national television! Zachary was five at the time, and he paid no attention to when the tape was rolling. He was concerned with a different kind of roll! Right in the middle of a pointed response I was making to one of Lesley's questions, he screamed from down the hall—second door on the left—"Mom! Mom! Somebody wipe me, would'ya!?"

CUT!!

During take two, Lesley asked me who my greatest inspiration was as a comedian. Of course I mentioned Minnie Pearl. But as the camera pulled back, I patted my mother on the knee and said, "But this lady is where I get most of my material. She is funny! She is joyful even in some tough days. This is my mother, Virginia, and I am proud of her because she is battling breast cancer and she's winning."

Just then Mother held up her hands and said, "Oh, stop! Stop right there, honey! Can we do this part all over again?" The entire staff—two cameramen, a lighting director, Lesley, the producer, and the hair and makeup woman—all had the most confused (and disappointed) looks on their faces. (I think the object is to get the interview done without wasting too much video footage.) Even with all the confusion (most of my neighbors and the women from Mother's church were peering through the picture window), we all thought we had really captured this moment on film. But Mother, for some reason, thought we should do it differently.

The producer said, "Stop tape." Then he ever-so-kindly turned to Mother and said, "Is there something wrong, Mrs. Farless?"

Mother looked at me, very serious and pale, and said, "Honey, you shouldn't say *breast* on national TV. That's just not nice."

After we picked the cameramen up off the floor, we started over. We tried to capture the moment again, but it never worked as well because we kept remembering Mother's innocent comments, and we couldn't stop laughing! I told you, Mother really is funny!

A Visit to the Cemetery

Several days later, Mother called, wanting me to take part in her little ritual: a visit to the cemetery. It is a ritual I'm not sure I understand, but it is important to Mother, so I go. It's not at all that I mind spending a few dollars for flowers. And I don't mind the drive there or the amount of time it takes for this ritual. And I certainly don't mind a visit or two on special occasions. Placing flowers at Charlotta and Cheralyn's graves is one thing, but having a picnic complete with fried chicken and potato salad—well, that's just a bit much for me. It seems that passing the KFC bucket around is a real reminder that they are not here, sitting in our circle. It is a reminder that they are gone—there in the ground. Dead. Cold. Gone. I don't like those reminders. I like placing flowers in their favorite colors in the church, commemorating their birthdays and their favorite seasons. Those are living memorials, and I like that best. I'm just weird, I guess!

Despite my own preferences on the matter, when Mother calls and wants to make that drive (picnic) to Forest Hill, I try to make sure she doesn't go alone. At this particular time in Mother's life—physically struggling through chemotherapy—I wasn't sure it was a good idea to hang out in the cemetery. It's hard enough to go to those two heart-shaped granite slabs with your last name printed across the front, but to go when you are facing an uphill battle with cancer—that's just not a real encouraging place to hang out.

I tried my best to suggest another day, but for some reason or other she needed to go today. "You know, Mom, we'll have better weather tomorrow."

"I know," she said, "but I've already made the potato salad for the grandkids." What could I say!

I picked up Mom and then we stopped for my two nephews, Josh (then age 15) and Jacob (age 10), who piled into the van with my kids, and we all headed to the cemetery. We made our normal stop at the little market in town that sold small potted plants and bought some red geraniums and some cut daisies, then on to KFC for original recipe (all white meat), and finally headed to the top of the hill where Cheralyn and Charlotta are buried.

After a difficult month of chemotherapy, Mother had lost all of her hair and her immune system was quite compromised, so we made her agree not to stay in the wind for too long. We climbed out of the van and made our way across the grounds, stopping once in awhile to take a look at the names of new markers draped with fresh-cut flowers left from recent funeral services.

As we made our way through the garden of granite statues, a gust of wind whipped up, taking with it a few of our newly pur- chased daisies—and Mother's newly purchased hair! Her Eva Gabor went rolling across the grass like a tumble weed. We all stopped dead still (bad choice of words, for a cemetery!). We were speechless. I knew how embarrassed Mother was about her hair loss. From that point on, everything seemed to move in slow motion.

And isn't it funny how each personality is clearly displayed when disaster strikes? My daughter Chera Kay is so quiet and sensitive. She grabbed Mother's hand and whispered, "It's okay, Nanny. It's okay."

Jacob, my younger nephew, stood motionless with the brightest red face, as if all his grandmother's clothes had been blown off with her hair.

Joshua, the oldest of Mother's grandchildren, is very athletic and very quiet. He simply took off and made the chase across the cemetery to retrieve the rolling bundle.

And my son, Zachary, who does have the slightest tendency to take after his mother, fell to the ground and rolled in the grass laughing. (So much for the strong, sensitive type!)

I certainly wanted to remain sensitive to Mother's embarrassment, but I couldn't help but blurt out, "Hey, Mother, you look like Yoda! I love that movie!" (I told you Zachary was a bit like his mother!)

Mother took off in pursuit (more like a shuffle) behind Joshua. She called out to me over her shoulder, "Are you going to help me or not?" Joshua finally snagged the bundle, turned and handed it to her without even looking up, much like a quarterback making a discreet hand-off. I caught up with her and took hold of one side of the wig as she took the other. Together we pulled it onto her head before any cars could drive by. The once nicely coifed Eva Gabor was now twisted and matted with grass and had lost all its glamour. The name of a certain television evangelist came to mind. (But I didn't say a word! Aren't you proud of me!?)

Mother made her way back to the heart-shaped headstone at Cheralyn's grave. She sat down there, her head in one hand, her arm outstretched and resting against the headstone at Charlotta's grave. Her small, round shoulders were quaking and shaking. *She is so embarrassed*, I thought, feeling bad that I had laughed earlier. *What do I say to her?* Her shoulders were still moving up and down as her grandchildren gathered in close around her. Even Zachary was quiet and concerned now. Finally, she lifted her face, revealing to us not tears of embarrassment but a face that glowed with laughter. She could hardly catch her breath—she was laughing so hard. Her laughter was contagious and one by one we all joined her.

Where There's Peace, There's Laughter

By watching my mother's life, I have learned that laughter doesn't leave us for good! Colossians 1:17 tells us, "He is before all things, and in him all things hold together." Ask my mother, she'll tell you it's the truth. She has shown me (not just told me) that when our relationship with God is intact, there is always that settled peace. Relationship—that's the key. There is no substitute for the peace that a relationship with Christ offers. And where there is peace, laughter abounds!

St. Augustine prayed: God, "you are more intimate to me than I am to myself." Moving to an intimate walk with the Lord through the power of the Holy Spirit helps us find the fun—even after the darkest days.

While wading through my dark days, I discovered some tangible relationship-building activities to pass the time. Can I share a few of those with you?

1. I journal. I actually write down conversations with myself, with my sisters, and most of the time, conversations with God.

2. I also use a lot of Post-it notes. Not simply to remind myself to buy laundry detergent, but to remind myself of promises in the Word of God. Which means you need to study the Word of God— find your own Post-it note promises and encouraging verses and litter your house with them.

3. I (we) listen to Christian music. (And turn the TV off.) Fortunately, my kids don't know any other music exists. (So don't tell them!) We lean into lyrics that uplift and remind us that we are not alone.

4. And what may seem to be the toughest tip for you: Praise the Lord! Praise the Lord? you say. Even in the tough times? Even when time is ticking so slowly that you think you will be in this valley forever? Yes, especially then. So are you wondering where God

is? Praise him and you'll see. Our God loves to hear his children loving him.

Remember Colossians 3: "Let the word of Christ dwell in you richly as you teach and admonish one another with all wisdom, and as you sing psalms, hymns and spiritual songs with gratitude in your hearts to God. And whatever you do, whether in word or deed, do it all in the name of Jesus, giving thanks to God the Father through him" (verses 16–17).

When we are seeking after the joy of his heart—then we laugh. We laugh in the right place, at the right time. God's perfect timing! To me, God's grace is that incredible element in our lives that allows us to somehow pass through devastation, poverty, embarrassment, heartache, or grief and somehow—in his time— stand on the other side grinning, because his "grace is sufficient" for me (2 Corinthians 12:9).

Be encouraged, because I've seen joy return again and again. I've watched the tears—but I've also heard the laughter! In my collection are the laughs of those who have suffered the loss of home, the pain of abuse, the anguish of divorce, the loneliness of rejection, and even the loss of a child. They are testaments that his grace is indeed sufficient, and they have found joy and laughter once again—sometimes after believing it was gone forever.

My collection of laughs continues; the bag is wonderfully heavy. And I believe that laughter is the indication that life will go on—the darkness will pass. I have seen God's sweet hands of mercy and grace brush away fears and been there when "rejoicing comes in the morning" (Psalm 30:5).

I saw it again that day in the cemetery as Mother, surrounded by her family, raised her hands in the air and shouted, "Well, praise the Lord! I guess as long as I can chase my hair, I am alive!"

And we laughed.

Epilogue

The Last Laugh

I really enjoy watching people. I know this may sound a bit devious, but I sat all day at the mall one Christmas season watching the last-minute shoppers scramble. It was the best entertainment! It was so exhilarating to watch, probably because it was the first year I can remember in a long time I wasn't out there doing the scrambling. Okay, maybe I was gloating—but watching people is a big hobby of mine.

And I love to watch people in airports. Especially the reunions. I travel so often that the excitement has kind of worn off. Usually I'm met at the airport by the college kid who drives the parking lot shuttle bus, and it's not very exciting to hear someone say, "Let me help you with your bag, ma'am," like I'm some old lady needing help across the street. But I never get tired of watching reunions. A few come to mind:

A tall, lanky teenager strolled off the jetway into a huge bear hug from his waiting Grandpa. Just as Grandpa chuckled about the "air up there" a tear fell down both their cheeks.

A shrill child's voice yelled "Mommy, Mommy" as a girl in pigtails skipped into her mother's arms. Perhaps she'd been visiting relatives, or maybe it had been her weekend to stay with Daddy. Whatever the reason, the miles all vanished when she was smothered in the waiting arms of her mommy.

Businessmen carrying briefcases and portfolios spotted their last names written across a dry-erase board. Even though strangers held the placards, they met them with hearty handshakes. These reunions weren't as emotional as the others, but I still a sensed an expectancy that something new, something good, was about to happen.

In the Chicago airport a tall woman, older than I, paced back and forth in front of the open jetway door. Most of the passengers had already deplaned—but still she waited—peering down an empty corridor. She sighed and glanced at her watch several times, still no sign of "her party." Had he/she/they missed the flight? Decided not to come? Finally, finally, I heard a squeaking sound I'd heard in airports before: a wheelchair. I watched as a flight attendant pushing a wheelchair came into view giving an elderly woman who held a purse in her lap a ride. The woman in the chair smiled at the sight of the one waiting for her. She stretched forth a feeble hand and said, "There she is. There's my little girl!" A wave of relief spread across the face of the waiting woman. She went to her and bent down to hug her neck. "Hi, Mom. I was beginning to worry about you."

Yes, I love reunions. The wait. The anticipation. The rewards. At the appointed hour—at just the right time—someone stands with arms wide open and a smile. In that moment, the space, the time in-between, vanishes in the sweetness of the reunion.

My kids are growing up so fast. No longer can I bring home small bags of peanuts, tiny bottles of shampoo, or cute little mending kits, and act as if I really brought them something special from my trip. Whenever I try to slip them something with "American Airlines" stamped on the package, Chera just rolls her eyes and Zachary complains. But I still think they're glad to see me when I get home. Chera hugs my waist, and Zach hugs my leg. We'll toss the peanuts and head to McDonald's for a happy meal. It's a good reunion.

There's another reunion I really look forward to—when we all get to heaven. Before Jesus left this earth he said, "I am going there to prepare a place for you . . . that you also may be where I am" (John 14:2–3). Wow! Did you hear that? He's preparing a reunion party. In the meantime he has not left us comfortless (see John 14:18). He did not abandon us.

And when I get there, I will see my grandmother running to meet me (without a switch in her hand!). I will hear Papaw tell stories again. And I will see a mother point and say, "There they are! There they are!" and her two daughters will squeal with delight as they rush into the warm circle of her arms. Charlotta and Cheralyn will probably giggle, and Mother will probably laugh harder than she did the day her wig blew off in the cemetery. (And if I don't get a new laugh in heaven, that'll be me cackling the loudest!)

And it won't be long before we notice the Presence beaming at this reunion. We shall know immediately who he is. No scars will have to define him, no explanation or introduction will be necessary, for only one Person in the universe has that mixture of love and laughter in his eyes like that—Jesus. He will step beside us and we will feel his touch on our quaking shoulders and know that he is pleased by the sound of his children laughing.

And as we all stroll along the street toward home (Mother moving better than she has in years and Charlotta and Cheralyn just talking over one another because there is so much to tell), I will find an opportunity to say, "Hey, Lord, did you hear the one about the . . ."

> There is a time for everything, and a season
> for every activity under heaven:
> a time to be born and a time to die,
> a time to plant and a time to uproot,
> a time to kill and a time to heal,
> a time to tear down and a time to build,
> a time to weep and a time to laugh,
> a time to mourn and a time to dance,
> a time to scatter stones and a time to gather them,
> a time to embrace and a time to refrain,
> a time to search and a time to give up,
> a time to keep and a time to throw away,
> a time to tear and a time to mend,
> a time to be silent and a time to speak,
> a time to love and a time to hate,
> a time for war and a time for peace.

—Ecclesiastes 3:1–8

CHONDA PIERCE INFORMATION

For Adult Preacher's Kids International information contact:

Second Row Ministries
212 Corner Circle
Murfreesboro, TN 37128
615-848-5000
Fax: 615-848-0407
E-Mail: The2ndRow@aol.com
Website: www.chonda.org

For concert availabilities and management:

Michael Smith & Associates
1110 Brentwood Pointe
Brentwood, TN 37027
615-377-3647
Fax: 615-376-2169
E-Mail: MSmithOrg@aol.com